LOWEN B. HOLD

Hit The Road!

100 Fun Road Trip Games to Pass the Time

Contents

Introduction

Ready to transform your road trips from monotonous to marvelous? Me too!

Whether you're traveling with your kids, grandkids, nieces and nephews, or your church youth group, it can be a challenge to keep everyone occupied and off their phones between all those energy-drink-powered pit stops.

My name is Lowen B. Hold, and I'm your co-rider, so take a little trip with me!

I grew up in the 1970s and 1980s, and my childhood was filled with all kinds of vivid memories on road trips. Even though the United States spans over 3,000 miles from end-to-end, my dad always managed to plan vacations in the most remote, wilderness-upholstered corners of our great nation.

The farther away it was, the more my dad got excited about it.

So my summers were spent in our preferred beast of burden — a green Ford Country Squire station wagon. Powered by paper maps with impossible fold lines and, in a good year, a portable transistor radio to share among all four of us boys (very fancy, indeed), we saw the majesty of the American landscape firsthand. A couple of us even saw it backwards while sitting on top of suitcases in the wayback seat.

Needless to say, we had gobs of time to kill. Our mom was a real Johnny-on-the-spot at coming up with games that would keep us on our best behavior, most of the time anyway. My brothers and I came up with our first drinking-style road trip game in the summer of 1978. We called it "Everlasting DadStopper."

Every time we would hear our mom say to our dad, "Oh, Tohave, stop the car!", we would all pop in an Everlasting Gobstopper candy at the same time. The stop was usually an historical marker plaque on the side of the road, and it was never not funny to hear one of us try to read that plaque aloud with a gobstopper firmly in cheek.

That summer, we all had stomachaches by the time we got to San Antonio.

Yes, summers with the adventurous coupling of Tohave N. Hold and Please Hold were the stuff of cherished and hilarious memories.

I want to bring some of that old-school summer nostalgia back, don't you? That's why I wrote this book.

Inside, you'll find a veritable smorgasbord of games and activities to keep everyone entertained on your asphalt odyssey. Yes, even those testy teens who think they're just too cool for your school.

I've got your back with classic car games like "License Plate Game" and "I Spy," creative endeavors like "Storytelling Games" and "Origami Challenge," and so much more.

A Game for Every Traveler

Your mission — should you choose to accept it — is to supercharge your road trips with these easy-to-play, fun, and engaging games. I tossed in some old-school favorites along with some new gems to keep you entertained.

Whether you're a road trip rookie or a fancy, pinky-up cross-country connoisseur, this book is jam-packed with activities perfect for every traveler. These games will show up as engagement, creativity, and social interaction, which, in my early days was referred to as "normal life."

Prepare yourself to start learning new things about your darling little travel buddies.

Embrace the Journey

It turns out there are a few benefits of playing games on the open road, besides keeping the driver awake. Not only do games break up the monotony of long drives, but they also reduce stress, promote relaxation, encourage teamwork, and create lasting memories. It's like meditation on wheels, baby!

As an added bonus, your players will learn about geography, history, and other fascinating subjects so you get some homeschool credits, too (unless you actually are a homeschooler, in which case, well, you know…).

Road trips offer a golden opportunity for your road crew to unplug from technology and cultivate a heightened appreciation of the world that is always around us. Contrary to popular notions, it is, in fact, a very big world after all!

Get Ready to Hit the Road!

I designed this book for easy navigation to make it a quick reference on the road. Each chapter is simply dedicated to a different game and number, a little hat tip to the old math of my youth.

Most of these games require minimal equipment, making them perfect for on-the-go fun. But don't forget to pack some paper, pens and a clipboard or two. I've also included in each chapter helpful tips and variations to create a little more challenge and make the games last long enough to get to the next watering hole.

So, pack your bags, load up on snacks, grab your reading glasses, and hit the road!

Your adventure awaits!

Lowen B. Hold

HIT THE
ROAD!

CLASSIC GAMES

Remember those days when we could amuse ourselves for hours on end without a screen in sight? Those righteous analog games only needed your friends, your family, and your imagination.

This chapter is loaded with timeless classics that'll totally bring back some major memories. These are the iconic games that have survived the test of time and are still a hit with kiddos and grown-ups alike.

From classic brain teasers like "I Spy" and "20 Questions" to the epic face-offs in "Rock-Paper-Scissors" and "Tic-Tac-Toe," these old-school favorites are guaranteed to send you on a wicked trip down memory lane and make some new memories for the next generation.

1. I Spy

Instructions:

1. One player, known as the "spy," selects an object from the surroundings without revealing it to the other players. The object can be inside the car or visible from the car, such as a billboard, a specific car color, or a landmark.
2. The spy starts the game by saying, "I spy with my little eye, something that is…" followed by a descriptive clue about the chosen object, such as its color, shape, or another characteristic. For example, "I spy with my little eye, something that is red."
3. The other players take turns guessing what the object might be based on the given clue. The spy can only answer "yes" or "no" to each guess.
4. The game continues until a player correctly identifies the object. That player then becomes the next spy and starts a new round.

Tips:

- Encourage the spy to be creative with their clues. Instead of just giving the color or shape, they can provide more abstract or less obvious hints, such as the object's function or its relation to other objects in the environment.
- Set a limit to the number of guesses each player can make per round, making it more challenging and encouraging players to think carefully before making a guess.
- Introduce a point system where players earn points for correct guesses, and keep track of each player's score throughout the road trip. The player with the highest score at the end of the trip is declared the "I Spy" champion.
- For a more challenging variation, play "I Spy" with only moving objects, such as other vehicles, pedestrians, or animals.
- If playing with younger children, consider simplifying the game by focusing on specific categories, such as colors or shapes, to help them understand the game more easily.

2. 20 Questions

Number of players: 2 or more
Objective: To guess the chosen object, person, or place by asking
a series of yes-or-no questions, testing players' deductive
reasoning and general knowledge

Instructions:

1. One player, known as the "thinker," selects an object, person, or place without revealing it to the other players. It can be anything from a famous person to a landmark or an everyday item.
2. The other players take turns asking yes-or-no questions to try to deduce what the thinker has chosen. The thinker can only answer "yes," "no," or "I don't know" to each question.
3. The players have a total of 20 questions to guess the chosen object, person, or place. If a player guesses correctly, they become the next thinker and start a new round.
4. If the players are unable to guess the chosen object, person, or place after 20 questions, the thinker reveals the answer and starts a new round as the thinker again.

Tips:

- Encourage the thinker to choose topics that are relevant to the road trip or the current surroundings to add a local flavor to the game.
- For a more challenging variation, limit the number of questions to fewer than 20 or require that players ask their questions in a specific order (e.g., starting with general questions and moving to more specific ones).
- Introduce a point system where players earn points for correct guesses or for the number of questions they ask before guessing correctly. Keep track of each player's score throughout the road trip, and declare the player with the highest score at the end of the trip the "20 Questions" champion.
- If playing with younger children, consider simplifying the game by focusing on specific categories, such as animals or vehicles, to help them understand the game more easily.

3. Rock-Paper-Scissors

```
Number of players: 2
Objective: To outwit your opponent by choosing the winning hand
symbol in a best-of-three or best-of-five series
```

Instructions:

1. Both players stand facing each other, with their hands in a fist, ready to play.
2. Players count down together, saying, "Rock, Paper, Scissors, Shoot!" On the word "Shoot," both players simultaneously make one of the following hand symbols:
   - Rock: A clenched fist
   - Paper: An open hand, fingers extended
   - Scissors: A fist with the index and middle fingers extended, forming a V shape
3. The winner of each round is determined by the following rules:
   - Rock crushes Scissors (Rock wins)
   - Scissors cuts Paper (Scissors wins)
   - Paper covers Rock (Paper wins)
4. If both players choose the same symbol, the round is a tie, and no points are awarded.
5. Play a predetermined number of rounds, such as best-of-three or best-

of-five, to determine the overall winner.

Tips:

- Introduce a point system, awarding one point for each round won. Keep track of each player's score throughout the road trip, and declare the player with the highest score at the end of the trip the "Rock-Paper-Scissors" champion.
- Add a creative twist by assigning road trip-themed hand symbols, such as:
  - Car (a steering wheel gesture)
  - Road (an extended arm, mimicking a straight road)
  - Tree (an arm bent at a 90-degree angle, like a tree branch)
- Create new winning rules for these symbols, and play as you would with the traditional game.

4. Tic-Tac-Toe

Number of players: 2
Objective: To get three Xs or Os in a row, either horizontally,
vertically, or diagonally

Instructions:

1. Draw a 3x3 grid on a piece of paper or use a pre-drawn game board.
2. One player takes X and the other takes O.
3. The first player places their chosen symbol on any empty square on the grid.
4. The second player then places their chosen symbol on any empty square on the grid.
5. The game continues in this manner, with players taking turns until one player has three of their symbols in a row, either horizontally, vertically, or diagonally.
6. If all nine squares are filled without either player achieving three in a row, the game is a draw and neither player wins.

Tips:

- A good strategy is to try and get the middle square, giving you more options to create a line of three.
- If you see your opponent is about to get three in a row, put your mark in the square they need to block them.
- A fork is a situation where a player has two opportunities to get three in a row (two non-blocked lines of two). Try to create forks and prevent your opponent from doing so.

5. Build a Sandcastle

Number of players: 2 or more
Objective: To guess a secret word or phrase before the sandcastle
is completely built

Instructions:

1. One player thinks of a word or phrase and writes down dashes to represent each letter of the word. For example, if the word is "apple," they would write "_ _ _ _ _."

2. The other players take turns guessing a letter that might be in the word.

3. If the guessed letter is in the word, the first player writes the letter in the appropriate blank space(s) to show where it appears in the word. For example, if the guessed letter is "p," the first player would write "_ p p _ _" on the paper.

4. If the guessed letter is not in the word, the first player draws one part of the "sandcastle," beginning with the base of the castle.

5. For each incorrect guess, add a new element to the sandcastle: a tower, a second tower, third tower, the door, windows on each tower, the flag on the first tower, the flag on the second tower, and finally, the flag on the third tower.

6. The game continues until one of the other players either correctly guesses the word, or the sandcastle is fully drawn and the game is lost.

Tips:

- Tailor your word or phrase choices to the theme of the road trip. If you're on a road trip to a national park, for example, choose words and phrases related to nature or the outdoors.
- If you have a larger group, split into two teams. Each team can take turns guessing the letters for a word or phrase thought up by the other team.
- To keep the game fresh, you can change the drawing to something else, like a picnic scene or a beach umbrella. This will also help to make the game adaptable to different ages and interests.
- Introduce small prizes or rewards for the winning player or team. This could be choosing the next song on the car stereo, picking the next pit stop for a snack, or even just gaining the title of "Sandcastle Guru" until the next game.

6. Connect the Dots

Number of players: 2 or more
Objective: To connect as many dots as possible and create the most boxes

Instructions:

1. Draw a grid of dots on a piece of paper, with at least 20 dots in total. The dots should be evenly spaced apart from each other.
2. The first player selects a dot and connects it with a line to another dot that is horizontally or vertically adjacent to it.
3. Using a different color pen or a colored pencil, the second player then takes their turn, selecting a dot and connecting it to another dot with a line.
4. Players take turns until one of them completes the fourth side of a square or box.
5. When a player completes a box, they write their initial inside it and get an extra turn.
6. The game continues until all boxes are completed.
7. The player with the most boxes at the end of the game wins.

Tips:

- Try to block your opponent from completing boxes by connecting dots that prevent them from closing off a square.
- Add a time limit to connect the dots. This increases the pressure and makes the game more challenging.
- Include some bonus dots that, if connected correctly, form an additional smaller image within the main one.

7. Spot the Difference

Number of players: 2 or more
Objective: To find the differences between two similar pictures

Instructions:

1. Before the trip, take at least two pictures each of various locations and load them to your phone or tablet. (It's okay to use your screen for this one because printer ink is like liquid gold!)
2. From your collection, choose two similar pictures or images.
3. Give everyone a few minutes to study the pictures and try to identify the differences.
4. Once everyone has had enough time to look at the pictures, cover one of the pictures or move it out of sight.
5. Players must then try to identify the differences between the two pictures.
6. The first player to correctly identify a difference gets a point.
7. Play continues until all differences have been identified or until a predetermined number of rounds have been played.

Tips:

- Set a time limit for spotting differences. The faster pace will make the game more challenging.
- In addition to differences, include some similarities that need to be spotted.
- Introduce a hint system where players can get clues, but at the cost of points.

8. Alphabet Game (General Edition)

Instructions:

1. Decide on a category for the game, such as "animals," "foods," or "movies."
2. The first player starts by saying a word that starts with the letter "A" that fits the category. For example, if the category is "animals," the first player could say "alligator."
3. The next player must then come up with a word that starts with the letter "B" and fits the category. For example, "bird."
4. Play continues in this manner, with each player taking turns coming up with a word that starts with the next letter of the alphabet that fits the category.
5. If a player can't think of a word that fits the category for their turn or repeats a word that has already been used, they are out of the game.
6. The last player remaining who comes up with a valid word when their turn comes wins the game.

Tips:

- To make the game more challenging, set a time limit for each round or require that each word must be a certain number of letters long.
- Make a rule that words must have two consecutive letters from the alphabet (like "apple" for "A," "bubble" for "B").
- Challenge players to come up with the longest word they can think of for each letter.
- To make the game easier for younger children, allow them to use any word that starts with the correct letter.

9. Simon Says

Number of players: Two or more
Objective: To be the last player remaining by only following the
instructions that begin with "Simon Says"

Instructions:

1. Assign one player as "Simon." This person will be responsible for giving out instructions.
2. The rest of the players face Simon and are required to follow Simon's instructions, but only when prefaced by the phrase "Simon says."
3. For example, if Simon says, "Simon says touch your nose," then all players should touch their nose. But if Simon just says, "Wave your arms," without saying "Simon says" first, players should not wave their arms.
4. Anyone who performs an action without hearing "Simon says" beforehand is out of the game.
5. The game continues until only one player is left. This person is declared the winner and usually becomes "Simon" for the next round.

Tips:

- Increase the speed of the commands to make the game more challenging. The faster Simon gives the commands, the harder it is for players to keep up and stay focused.
- Give two commands at once, such as "Simon says touch your nose and tap your feet." This increases the difficulty and keeps players on their toes.
- Just for giggles, include commands like "Simon says act like a monkey" or "Simon says pretend you're an airplane."

10. Audio Red Light, Green Light

Number of players: 2 or more
Objective: To react quickly to calls and perform tasks without
making a mistake

Instructions:

1. Choose one player to be the navigator, who will give commands to other players. The navigator can sit anywhere in the car.
2. The other players will listen attentively to the navigator's commands and prepare to perform specific tasks.
3. The navigator will call out "Green light!" to signal the other players to start the task (it could be anything like drawing, writing, singing, counting, or any activity that doesn't disturb the driver).
4. The players will continue their task as long as the navigator says "Green light!".
5. The navigator can call out "Red light!" at any time, at which point the players must stop their task immediately.
6. If a player is caught still performing the task after the navigator has called out "Red light!", they get a penalty point.
7. The navigator will resume calling out "Green light!" and "Red light!" until one player completes the task first without any penalty points. That player becomes the navigator for the next round.

Tips:

- The tasks can be simple ones like counting, singing, or more challenging ones like solving a riddle or a puzzle.
- Control the difficulty of the game by adjusting the speed of the "Red Light" and "Green Light" calls. The quicker the transitions, the harder the game will be.
- Be creative with penalties. Instead of just adding a point, maybe the penalized player has to tell a joke, do a funny impression, or make funny faces.
- Consider implementing a points system where players earn points for completing tasks first or lose points for moving during "Red Light."

11. Charades

Number of players: 2 or more
Objective: To guess the word or phrase acted out by the player

Instructions:

1. One player begins the game by choosing a word or phrase and keeping it secret from the other players.
2. The player then acts out the word or phrase using only body language and gestures, without speaking or making any sounds.
3. The other players watch the acting and try to guess what the word or phrase is.
4. Players may ask yes-or-no questions to help them guess, but the player acting out the word or phrase may not respond verbally.
5. The first player to correctly guess the word or phrase gets a point and becomes the next player to act out a word or phrase.
6. The game continues with each player taking turns to act out words or phrases and guess what others are acting out.

Tips:

- To add some extra fun and challenge to the game, you could introduce themed rounds. For example, you could have a round dedicated to movies from the '80s, a round for famous celebrities, or a round for popular songs.
- Make it a rapid-fire round where the actor has to act out as many words as they can in a limited time.
- While traditional charades does not use props, adding them can increase the fun factor significantly. You could use hats, scarves, or other items that can help players act out their clues more effectively.
- Allow two people to act out the charade together. This can lead to more complex and entertaining performances.

12. Telephone

Number of players: 4 or more
Objective: To pass a message along a line of players and see how
much it changes from the original message

Instructions:

1. The players should sit or group up with enough distance between them
   so that they cannot hear each other's whispers.
2. The first player thinks of a phrase or sentence and whispers it to the
   person next to them.
3. That person then whispers what they heard to the next person in the
   line, and so on until the message reaches the last person in the line.
4. The last person in the line then says out loud what they heard, and the
   original message is revealed.
5. Compare the original message to the final message that was heard and
   see how much it has changed.
6. The game can be repeated with a new message and the players can switch
   positions in the line to give everyone a chance to start the message.

Tips:

- It's important to whisper the message so that the other players can't hear it.
- Add background noise or music to increase the challenge of hearing the message correctly.
- To make the game more challenging, start with a longer sentence, or include more complex words. This will make it harder for players to remember the exact wording.
- Create a theme for each round (e.g., movie titles, famous quotes, song lyrics). This adds a fun twist to the game and allows players to be even more creative with their interpretations.
- Try a version of the game where the message is mimed rather than whispered.

13. Guess the Animal

Number of players: 2 or more
Objective: To correctly guess the animal by asking yes-or-no
questions

Instructions:

1. One player thinks of an animal and keeps it secret from the other players.
2. The other players take turns asking yes-or-no questions about the animal. For example, "Does it live in the water?" or "Is it a carnivore?"
3. The player who thought of the animal can only answer "yes" or "no" to the questions.
4. The players continue asking questions until someone thinks they know the animal.
5. The player who thinks they know the animal can make a guess. If they are correct, they get to go next and think of a new animal. If they are incorrect, play continues with the other players asking more questions.
6. The game can continue for as long as the players want, with each player taking turns thinking of an animal for the others to guess.

Tips:

- Exclude common animals like cats, dogs, horses, etc. from the guessing game. This forces players to think beyond the usual suspects.
- Limit the number of questions a player can ask before making a guess. This encourages strategic thinking.
- Make it a timed game. The player who guesses the animal within the shortest time is the winner.
- If your group is into biology, using scientific names for the animals can make the game more difficult and educational.

14. Slug Bug

Number of players: 2 or more
Objective: To be the first one to spot a Volkswagen Beetle (or "Bug") and say "Slug Bug" before anyone else does

Instructions:

1. All players should keep their eyes peeled for any Volkswagen Beetles (classic or newer ones) they spot on the road.
2. As soon as a player spots a Beetle, they should say "Slug Bug" out loud and indicate the color of the Beetle.
3. Once a "Slug Bug" has been called, no other player can call it for that same car.
4. The player who first calls "Slug Bug" for a particular Beetle earns a point.
5. Play continues until the end of the road trip or a predetermined score limit is reached.

Tips:

- Make the game more challenging by assigning different point values to different colored Beetles. For example, commonly spotted colors like black or silver might be worth one point, while rarer colors like yellow or pink could be worth more points.

- Try adding some rules. For example, you could institute a penalty for falsely identifying a car as a Slug Bug.
- To make it more interesting, you can extend the game to include other classic or unique car models.

15. Quiet Game

Number of players: 2 or more
Objective: To remain quiet for as long as possible

Instructions:

1. One player is chosen to start the game as the "Quiet Game Leader."
2. The Quiet Game Leader announces the start of the game by saying "Go!" or a similar word or phrase.
3. From that moment on, everyone in the car must remain silent. No talking, laughing, or making noise of any kind is allowed.
4. The last person to remain quiet wins the game.
5. If someone breaks the silence, they are out of the game and must be silent for the remainder of the round.
6. The Quiet Game Leader can declare a winner at any time, but typically the game continues until everyone has been eliminated except for one person.
7. The winner becomes the Quiet Game Leader for the next round.

Tips:

- If a player wants to communicate, they must mime their message. This adds an element of charades to the game and increases the fun factor.
- To make the game more exciting, use a timer. The person who remains quiet the longest within a set time limit wins.
- Players can get creative with how they remain quiet. Maybe they find a way to entertain themselves silently or help another passenger without making a noise. Reward points for these creative endeavors.

WORD GAMES

This collection of word games will make your next family road trip feel like an epic journey through the land of linguistic delights — or at least a bit less like a journey through the land of the lost.

From the legendary "License Plate Game (Letter Edition)" that'll have you hunting for alphabet soup on wheels, to the mind-bending "Word Ladder Game" that'll take your wordy wit to new heights, these games are guaranteed to keep you and your travel crew hooked.

So rally your word-warrior roadsters (even the self-professed word game haters) and get ready to roll!

Just don't forget to pack a pen and paper – you'll need it to keep score and track your word-conquering progress as you play!

16. License Plate Game (Letter Edition)

Number of players: 2 or more
Objective: To spot license plates with the letters of the
alphabet in order, from A to Z

Instructions:

1. Each player should have a pen or pencil and a piece of paper.
2. Begin the game by looking for a license plate with a letter "A."
3. Once a license plate with an "A" is spotted and confirmed by the other players, move on to "B."
4. Continue in this way through the alphabet, in order, until you reach "Z."
5. Remember, the letters must be spotted in order, so even if you see a "Z," you cannot call it out until you have spotted all the other letters up to "Z."
6. The first player to spot "Z" wins the game.

Tips:

- For a more challenging game, the players have to find the letters in the license plates in order but also numbers 0-9 after completing the alphabet.

- If you are playing in a group, you can split into teams and compete against each other, with each team trying to spot the alphabet in order on license plates before the other team.
- For a variation, you could require the letters to be the first letter on the plate or the last letter.

17. Secret Word Game

```
Number of players: 2 or more
Objective: To guess the secret word before the number of chances
run out
```

Instructions:

1. Choose a secret word that everyone playing the game is familiar with.
2. Write dashes representing each letter of the secret word on a piece of paper.
3. Assign a number of chances to guess the secret word, depending on the difficulty of the word and the age of the players.
4. One player thinks of the secret word and tells the other players how many letters it contains.
5. The other players take turns guessing a letter that might be in the word. If the letter is in the word, the player who thought of the secret word writes the letter in its correct position on the dashes. If the letter is not in the word, one chance is used up.
6. Players can also guess the whole word at any point in the game.
7. If the players guess the secret word correctly before the number of chances run out, they win the game. If not, the player who thought of the secret word wins.

Tips:

- As the game goes on, increase the difficulty of the secret word. It could start as a single, easy word and evolve into phrases or more obscure words.
- If the secret word isn't guessed after a certain number of tries, the person who chose it should provide a clue.
- Allow each player to choose a secret word at the start of the game. This can add more confusion and excitement to the game as players have multiple words to guess.

18. Word Association Game

Number of players: 2 or more
Objective: To say a word that is associated with the previous
player's word and continue the chain as long as possible

Instructions:

1. The first player says a word, any word that comes to their mind.
2. The second player then says a word that is associated with the first player's word.
3. The third player says a word that is associated with the second player's word, and so on.
4. The game continues until someone is unable to come up with a new associated word or until a predetermined time limit is reached.
5. The last player to successfully come up with a word wins.

Tips:

- To add an extra layer of challenge, establish a theme at the start of the game. This could be anything from a specific category like "animals" or "movies" to a broader theme like "summer" or "vacation." Players would then have to associate their words strictly within this theme, making the game a test of both quick thinking and thematic knowledge.

- For a faster-paced game, introduce a time limit for responses. This could be a countdown of 5 or 10 seconds. If a player can't think of an associated word within the time limit, they're out of the game.

19. Reverse Alphabet Game (Foods Edition)

Instructions:

1. Decide who will go first.
2. The first player must come up with a food item that starts with the letter "Z." They can take as much time as they need, but if they can't think of anything, the turn passes to the next player.
3. The next player must come up with a food item that starts with the letter "Y." The game continues in this way, with each player taking a turn to come up with a food item that starts with the next letter of the alphabet in reverse order.
4. If a player can't think of a food item, they can either skip their turn or ask the other players for help.
5. The game ends when a player successfully comes up with a food item that starts with the letter "A."

Tips:

- Introduce different cuisines as rounds (Italian, Mexican, etc.). Players must come up with food items only from those cuisines, testing their culinary knowledge.
- Allow only food items that contain a specific ingredient, such as "chocolate" or "cheese."
- Break up the game into different rounds for breakfast, lunch, dinner, and dessert items. This can challenge players to think of foods appropriate for each mealtime.

20. Reverse Alphabet Game (Animals Edition)

Number of players: 2 or more
Objective: To name animals in reverse alphabetical order until
someone cannot think of an animal to name

Instructions:

1. The first player names an animal that begins with the letter "Z."
2. The next player must name an animal that begins with the letter "Y."
3. Play continues in this manner, with each player naming an animal in reverse alphabetical order until someone cannot think of an animal to name.
4. Once a player is unable to name an animal, they are out of the game.
5. The game continues until only one player is left standing.

Tips:

- Play rounds based on different habitats like jungle, ocean, desert, etc. The animals named should belong to the given habitat.
- Dedicate a round to endangered animals to raise awareness and learn about these species.

- If a player can accurately mimic the sound of the animal they name, they get an extra point or advantage in the next round.

21. Reverse Alphabet Game (Cities Edition)

Number of players: 2 or more
Objective: To name a city starting with each letter of the
alphabet in reverse order

Instructions:

1. The first player starts by naming a city that begins with the letter "Z."
2. The next player must then name a city that begins with the letter "Y," and so on, in reverse alphabetical order.
3. If a player cannot think of a city within 10 seconds, they are out of the game.
4. The game continues until only one player remains, or until the group has gone through the entire alphabet.

Tips:

- Make each round about a different continent. This can increase the game's difficulty and educate players about world geography.
- For each city named, the player should also name a famous landmark from that city.

- Challenge players to only name cities with populations over a certain number (e.g., one million residents).

22. Reverse Alphabet Game (TV Shows Edition)

Number of players: 2 or more
Objective: To be the last player standing by correctly naming a
TV show that starts with the given letter before the time runs out

Instructions:

1. Decide on a category for the game, in this case, TV shows.
2. The first player says a TV show that starts with the letter "Z."
3. The next player must then name a TV show that starts with the letter "Y."
4. The game continues in this way, with each player naming a TV show that starts with the next letter of the alphabet in reverse order.
5. Players have a set amount of time to come up with a TV show. If they cannot name a show in time or name one that does not fit the category, they are out of the game.
6. The last player standing wins the game.

Tips:

- Dedicate each round to TV shows from a specific decade. This can test players' knowledge of pop culture history.
- Restrict each round to a specific genre like comedy, drama, or science fiction.
- When a player names a TV show, they should also name a character from that show. If they can't, they lose a turn or a point.

23. Reverse Alphabet Game (Movies Edition)

Number of players: 2 or more
Objective: To come up with a movie title that begins with each
letter of the alphabet in reverse order, starting with "Z" and
ending with "A"

Instructions:

1. Decide on a category, in this case, movies.
2. The first player says a movie title that begins with the letter "Z."
3. The second player then comes up with a movie title that begins with the letter "Y," and so on.
4. If a player cannot come up with a title, they are out of the game.
5. The game continues until one player is left standing or until the players decide to end the game.
6. To make the game more challenging, players can set a time limit for each turn or agree to only use movies from a certain time period or genre.

Tips:

- Break the game into rounds where you only name movies released in a certain decade, testing players' knowledge of film history.
- Restrict each round to a specific genre like action, romance, horror, etc. This can be an exciting challenge for movie buffs!
- If a player can name an actor from the movie they just mentioned, they get an extra point or a chance to skip a difficult letter.

24. Reverse Alphabet Game (Song Titles Edition)

```
Number of players: 2 or more
Objective: To be the last player to come up with a song title
that starts with the given letter
```

Instructions:

1. Decide on a category for the game, in this case, song titles.
2. The first player says a song title that starts with the letter "Z."
3. The next player must come up with a song title that starts with the letter "Y," and so on, until the letter "A" is reached.
4. If a player can't think of a song title that starts with the given letter, they are out of the game.
5. The game continues until there is only one player left, who is the winner.

Tips:

- Make each round about songs from a particular artist or band. This can make the game more challenging and fun especially if players are fans of different genres.
- Restrict the game to only songs that have made it to the Billboard Top

100. This way players will learn about popular music they may not know about.

- If a player can sing a line from the song they just mentioned they get an extra point or a chance to skip a difficult letter.

25. Reverse Alphabet Game (Authors Edition)

Number of players: 2 or more
Objective: To name an author whose last name starts with the next
letter of the alphabet in reverse order, starting from "Z" and
working backwards to "A"

Instructions:

1. Decide on a category of authors, such as "classic literature" or "modern fiction."
2. The first player starts by naming an author whose last name starts with the letter "Z."
3. The next player must name an author whose last name starts with the letter "Y," and so on, working backwards through the alphabet.
4. If a player cannot think of an author, they are out of the game.
5. The game continues until only one player is left.

Tips:

- Each round can be dedicated to authors known for a particular genre, like mystery, romance, fantasy, etc.
- In each round, players can only name authors from a specific country,

testing their knowledge of global literature.

- If a player can name a book by the author they just mentioned, they get an extra point or a chance to skip a difficult letter.

26. Spelling Bee Game

Instructions:

1. Choose a player to start as the Spelling Master.
2. The Spelling Master will say a word and the player to their left will have to spell it out loud.
3. If the player spells the word correctly, they remain in the game. If they spell it incorrectly, they are out of the game.
4. The Spelling Master continues to give words to each player in turn until there is only one player left, who is the winner.
5. If the Spelling Master runs out of words, they can use a dictionary or other resource to find more challenging words.

Tips:

- Include words that contain difficult or often misspelled letters, such as "ph," "kn," or "gh," to make the game more challenging.
- Select a theme for each round, such as medical terms, scientific terms, or words from different languages.

- Incorporate a time limit for each word to add a sense of urgency and excitement.
- For younger players, you can allow them to write the word down before spelling it out loud.

27. Categories Game

Number of players: 2 or more
Objective: To name items within a specific category until a
player cannot think of any more items

Instructions:

1. Choose a category, such as "colors," "fruits," or "animals."
2. The first player starts by naming an item within that category, such as "red."
3. The next player must name another item within the category that starts with the last letter of the previous item. For example, if the first player said "red," the second player could say "dragonfruit."
4. Play continues in this manner with each player taking turns naming items within the chosen category until a player cannot think of any more items.
5. The last player to name an item wins the round.
6. Choose a new category and start again.

Tips:

- Make the game more challenging by selecting narrow categories like "types of cheese" or "18th-century painters."
- Mix two categories for a round like "actors in action movies."
- For a fun twist include a wildcard round where players can choose their category.
- To make the game more challenging, set a time limit for each turn.

28. Movie Quote Game

Number of players: 2 or more
Objective: To correctly guess the movie from which a given quote
is taken

Instructions:

1. The first player selects a quote from a movie and says it out loud.
2. The other players try to guess which movie the quote is from.
3. If someone guesses correctly, they get a point.
4. If nobody guesses correctly after a set amount of time, the person who said the quote reveals the movie it's from.
5. The next player selects a quote and the game continues in the same way.

Tips:

- Divide the quotes by decade to test players' knowledge of classic and contemporary films.
- Require players to name the character who said the quote, not just the movie.
- For an added challenge, players could be required to continue the quote or provide the following line.

29. Name That Tune (with songs)

Number of players: 2 or more
Objective: To correctly guess the name of the song and/or the
artist before the other players

Instructions:

1. Choose one person to be the "DJ" for the round.
2. The DJ plays a short clip of a song.
3. The other players have to guess the name of the song and/or the artist.
4. The first player to correctly guess the name of the song and/or the artist gets a point.
5. If no one can guess the correct answer, the DJ can choose to play another clip from the same song or choose a new song altogether.
6. Rotate the role of the DJ to the next player and continue playing until everyone has had a chance to be the DJ or a predetermined number of rounds have been played.
7. The player with the most points at the end of the game is the winner.

Tips:

- Use cover versions of popular songs to test the players' real knowledge of the tune.
- Include TV show theme songs or commercial jingles for a fun twist.
- Separate rounds by genre to keep the game interesting and diverse.
- It may be helpful to establish some rules beforehand, such as the length of the song clip or whether partial credit is allowed for guessing only the artist or only the song title.

30. Word Ladder Game

Number of players: 2 or more
Objective: To create a word ladder by changing one letter of a word to make a new word until a target word is reached

Instructions:

1. Choose a target word, which will be the final word in the word ladder.
2. The first player starts by saying a word.
3. The next player must then say a word that differs by only one letter from the previous word. For example, if the first word was "cat," the next word could be "bat" or "cot."
4. Players take turns until the target word is reached.
5. If a player cannot think of a word or repeats a word that has already been said, they are out of the game.
6. The player who says the target word or the player who makes it the furthest along the word ladder wins.

Tips:

- Set a minimum length for the words to make the game more challenging.
- Require that each new word must begin with a later letter in the alphabet than the previous word.

- Make each ladder follow a theme, like "words associated with summer," to narrow down possible words and add a level of difficulty.
- Use a dictionary or online resource to settle any disputes over whether a word is valid or not.

31. Ghost

```
Number of players: 2 or more
Objective: To avoid completing a word while still challenging
your opponent to try and complete it
```

Instructions:

1. The first player starts the game by saying a letter. This will be the first letter of the word being spelled.
2. Players then take turns adding one letter at a time to create a word. The idea is to avoid completing a word. Each letter added must be part of a real word.
3. The game ends when a player completes a word of four letters or more on their turn. That player loses the round.
4. For example:
   - Player 1: "S"
   - Player 2: "T"
   - Player 1: "A"
   - Player 2: "R" (Player 2 completes the word "STAR" and loses this round)
5. Players usually play multiple rounds, and the player who loses the least number of rounds is the overall winner.
6. If a player believes that there is no word that starts with the current string of letters, they can challenge the previous player. If the challenged

player can't state a word that starts with the current string of letters, the challenged player loses. If the challenged player does state a word, the challenger loses.

7. For example:
   - Player 1: "T"
   - Player 2: "U"
   - Player 1: "A"
   - Player 2: "R"
   - Player 1: Challenges Player 2
   - (Player 1 wins the challenge, because there is no word starting with "TUAR")

Tips:

- Try to steer towards longer words. This gives you more room to maneuver and less chance of finishing a word.
- Increase difficulty by limiting the use of certain common letters.
- If the word seems to be leading towards an obvious conclusion, try to throw a curveball by adding a letter that shifts the direction of the word.
- Apply a time limit for each player's turn to keep the pace up.

32. Word Tennis

Number of players: 2 or more players
Objective: To keep a rally of words going back and forth between players without hesitation, repetition, or deviation

Instructions:

1. The first player begins by saying a word (e.g. "apple").
2. The second player responds with a word that starts with the last letter of the previous word (e.g. "elephant").
3. The first player then responds with a word that starts with the last letter of the previous word (e.g. "tiger").
4. Players continue going back and forth until a player hesitates, repeats a word, or deviates from the category (e.g. saying "raisins" instead of "rhinoceros").
5. The player who made the mistake loses that round, and the other player earns a point.
6. The game continues with players taking turns starting each round.
7. The player with the most points at the end of the game wins.

Tips:

- To make the game harder, you could make a rule that words must be of a certain number of letters.
- Add a time limit for each player to respond. If a player cannot come up with a word within the time limit, they lose the round.
- Make the game more complex by requiring the next word to start with the last letter of the word previous to the current one.
- Add a rule that words must be a certain length, like at least six letters.

33. Word Art Relay

Number of players: 2 or more
Objective: To visually represent words or phrases with drawings
so that other players can guess what they are

Instructions:

1. Each player needs a blank piece of paper and a set of markers or crayons.
2. The first player thinks of a word or phrase (it could be anything - an object, an animal, a place, etc.)
3. The player then has a set amount of time to draw the word or phrase on their paper without writing any words or numbers.
4. Once the time is up, they pass their drawing to the next player, who must guess what the drawing represents.
5. If the guess is correct, both the artist and the guesser get a point. If not, no points are awarded.
6. The game continues with each player taking turns to draw and guess. The player with the most points at the end of the game wins.

Tips:

- Instead of passing the drawing to be guessed, the next player could be asked to add onto the drawing with a concept of their own.
- Incorporate a speed round where players have to draw and guess within a limited timeframe.

34. Word Bingo

Number of players: 2 or more
Objective: To be the first player to fill out their bingo card by correctly guessing the listed words

Instructions:

1. Before starting the game, create bingo cards by drawing a 5x5 grid on a piece of paper and filling each square with a word.
2. The words can be related to a specific theme or category (e.g., animals, movies, famous people).
3. Choose one player to be the caller. The caller should have a list of the words used on the bingo cards.
4. The caller will randomly select a word from their list and read it out loud.
5. Each player will then check his or her bingo cards to see if they have the word listed.
6. If a player has the word on their card, they can mark it off.
7. The first player to mark off a full row (horizontal, vertical, or diagonal) shouts "Bingo!" and is declared the winner.

Tips:

- Make the game more challenging by using longer or less common words.
- To make the game last longer, require players to fill out the entire bingo card instead of just a row.
- For those learning a new language, play the game in that language.
- Add bonus squares that require the player to spell a word or answer a question related to the word to win the square.

35. Word Scramble

Instructions:

1. One player chooses a word and writes it down scrambled on an index card or piece of paper.
2. The player shows the scrambled word to the other players.
3. The other players have to unscramble the letters to form a real word.
4. The player who unscrambles the word first gets a point.
5. Players take turns to choose and scramble the words.
6. Set a time limit for each round (e.g., one minute) and keep track of the points.
7. The player with the most points at the end of the game wins.

Tips:

- Assign different points based on the length of the unscrambled word. The longer the word, the higher the points it might bring.
- Occasionally introduce a scrambled word with one or two extra letters that don't belong, making the task a little more difficult. Players will

have to figure out the unnecessary letters in addition to unscrambling the word.

- For an additional twist, once the word is unscrambled, players could be asked to come up with synonyms of the word.

36. Name That Thing

Number of players: 2 or more
Objective: To identify as many items in a specific category as
possible within a limited amount of time

Instructions:

1. Choose a category for the round, such as "animals," "movies," or "foods." The broader the category, the longer the game tends to last.
2. Decide on a time limit for each round, typically 1-2 minutes.
3. The first player names an item from the chosen category. For example, if the chosen category is "Animals," the first player might say "Elephant."
4. The next player must then name another thing within the category, but it must not be a repetition of anything previously said. For instance, they might say "Giraffe."
5. The game continues with players taking turns to name unique things within the chosen category.
6. If a player cannot think of anything new within the category or repeats a previous answer, they are out of the game.
7. The last player standing at the end of the round wins the round and earns a point.
8. Repeat for several rounds, changing the category for each round.
9. The player with the most points at the end of the game wins.

Tips:

- To make the game more challenging, you can limit the categories to more specific themes, such as "types of flowers" or "90s TV shows."
- For an additional challenge, introduce a "Sticky Letter Rule." In this version, the next thing named must start with the same letter that the last thing ended with. For instance, if the category is "Animals" and the first player says "Elephant," the next player might say "Tiger."

MEMORY GAMES

Get ready for razor-sharp recollections! We've got a list of brain-boosting games that'll turn long car rides into a memory-making marathon.

From the old-school delights of "Memory Match" to the more imaginative escapades of "Alphabet Memory Game," there's a memory challenge for everyone in the car.

Feeling like a storyteller? Dive into "I'm Going on a Picnic," where you'll need to remember and recite a growing list of picnic provisions.

Don't worry if your memory is rustier than a '70s station wagon, the "Name Game" will have you practicing while having a blast.

So buckle up and put your memory to the test!

37. Memory Game

Number of players: 2 or more
Objective: To remember and recall the maximum number of items
from a list of items

Instructions:

1. One person starts by saying a list of items, for example, "apple, book, cat, dog, elephant."
2. The next person then repeats the list and adds one more item, for example, "apple, book, cat, dog, elephant, fish."
3. The game continues with each person repeating the entire list and adding one more item each time.
4. If a player forgets an item, they are out of the game.
5. The game continues until only one player is left or until no one can remember the entire list.

Tips:

- Make a fun rhythm or song out of the items. Sing the list in a particular tune to help recall.
- Encourage players to repeat the list in their head after each turn to help with memory recall.

- Try to visualize the items or concepts in your mind. Mental images can be easier to remember than abstract ideas or words.
- Connect the items you're trying to remember by creating a story that involves them. This can help form a stronger memory of the items.

38. Memory Match

Number of players: 2 or more
Objective: To match the most pairs of cards

Instructions:

1. Shuffle a deck of cards and lay them all face down on a table or flat surface.
2. The first player flips over any two cards of their choice.
3. If the two cards match, the player takes them off the table or surface and keeps them.
4. If the two cards do not match, the player turns them back over, and it becomes the next player's turn.
5. The game continues with players taking turns until all the cards have been matched.
6. The player with the most pairs of cards at the end of the game is the winner.

Tips:

- Using themed decks (like Pokemon cards, Marvel characters, etc.) can make the game more interesting for younger travelers.
- Consider adding a time limit for each turn to make decision-making

more critical.

- Instead of a grid, scatter the cards randomly on the table or flat surface. This adds an extra level of difficulty as players can't rely on grid patterns to remember card locations.
- Try a round where players are not allowed to communicate or react to the cards being flipped. This tests each player's focus and memory without cues from others.

39. Road Sign Bingo

```
Number of players: 2 or more players
Objective: To spot the signs on your Bingo card in a row
horizontally, vertically, or diagonally
```

Instructions:

1. Before setting off on your road trip, create individual Bingo cards filled with images or names of different road signs you're likely to encounter along your route. For example, stop signs, yield signs, pedestrian crossing, highway markers, state line signs, animal crossing signs, speed limit signs, etc.
2. Distribute a Bingo card and a pen or marker to each player.
3. As you drive, players mark off the road signs on their Bingo card that they spot on the road.
4. The first player to call out "Bingo!" after completing a row wins the game.

Tips:

- Consider adding a "free space" in the center for an easier game.
- Add a twist to the game by including bonus points for rare signs, or by having "road sign challenges" where a player can earn an extra point by

correctly explaining what a certain road sign means.

40. License Plate Game (Memory Edition)

Instructions:

1. The first player starts by saying a license plate number out loud.
2. The second player then repeats the first license plate number and adds another license plate number to the sequence.
3. Each subsequent player must repeat the entire sequence of license plate numbers in the correct order and add another license plate number to the end of the sequence.
4. Players are eliminated if they forget the correct sequence of license plate numbers or repeat a license plate number that has already been said in the sequence.
5. The last player remaining is the winner.

Tips:

- Start with a shorter sequence of license plate numbers and gradually increase the length as players become more comfortable with the game.
- Encourage players to create a mnemonic device to help remember the

sequence of license plate numbers or associate the letters and numbers on the license plates with words or images.

82

41. I'm Going on a Picnic

Number of players: 3 or more
Objective: To remember and repeat a growing list of items in the
right order

Instructions:

1. The first player says, "I'm going on a picnic and I'm bringing…" and then chooses an item to bring, for example, "an apple."
2. The second player repeats the first player's sentence, including the item they brought, and then adds their own item to the list, for example, "I'm going on a picnic and I'm bringing an apple and a blanket."
3. The third player repeats the entire sentence, including the first two items, and then adds their own item to the list, for example, "I'm going on a picnic and I'm bringing an apple, a blanket, and a Frisbee^{TM}."
4. Players continue taking turns, repeating the entire list of items in order and adding their own item to the list.
5. If a player forgets an item, they are out of the game.
6. The game continues until there is only one player left, who is declared the winner.

Tips:

- To make the game more challenging, you can add a rule that all items must begin with the same letter or fall into a certain category (e.g. all food items or all items you would bring on a camping trip).
- You can also change the scenario of the picnic to fit a different theme or location, such as "I'm going on a road trip and I'm bringing…" or "I'm going on a hike and I'm bringing…"
- The game can be more entertaining if players come up with silly or surprising items to bring on a picnic. Just be sure they still fit the chosen category!

42. Picnic Game

Number of players: 3 or more
Objective: To remember and recite all of the items brought on a
picnic in alphabetical order

Instructions:

1. The first player begins by saying "I'm going on a picnic and I'm bringing (an item that begins with the letter 'A')." For example, "I'm going on a picnic and I'm bringing apples."
2. The next player repeats the first player's item and adds an item that begins with the letter "B." For example, "I'm going on a picnic and I'm bringing apples and bananas."
3. Each player continues reciting all of the previous items and adding a new item that begins with the next letter of the alphabet. For example, "I'm going on a picnic and I'm bringing apples, bananas, and a camera."
4. If a player forgets an item or repeats an item that has already been said, they are out of the game.
5. The game continues until all players have been eliminated, leaving only the winner.

Tips:

- To make the game more challenging, players can add additional restrictions to the items, such as specifying the type of food (e.g. fruit, snack, dessert) or requiring items to fit a certain theme (e.g. beach picnic, camping trip).
- To make the game easier for younger players, you can allow them to write down the items as they are said to help them remember.
- If you have a large group of players, you can divide them into teams and have each team work together to come up with the items in alphabetical order.

43. Name Game

Number of players: 3 or more
Objective: To come up with names starting with a given letter and
fitting specific criteria

Instructions:

1. The first player selects a letter and announces it to the group.
2. The second player then must come up with a name starting with the chosen letter (e.g. "Alice").
3. The third player must then come up with another name starting with the chosen letter but also including a specific criteria (e.g. "Beautiful Alice").
4. Play continues with each player adding a new name that starts with the chosen letter and fitting the given criteria until someone cannot come up with a name, at which point they are eliminated.
5. The last player remaining is declared the winner.

Tips:

- Set specific criteria or categories that will challenge players to come up with more unique and interesting names.
- For tough letters like "X" or "Q," decide on the rules beforehand whether

these can be skipped or require a valid name.

- Encourage players to use names from different cultures or languages to make the game more diverse and educational.
- Introduce a speed round where players have a time limit to keep the pace lively.

44. Alphabet Memory Game

Number of players: 2 or more
Objective: To remember the sequence of the alphabet by taking
turns reciting it and adding a new letter to the end

Instructions:

1. The first player begins by saying the letter "A." This sets the stage for the sequence that each player will have to remember and repeat.
2. The next player now recites the previously stated letter, "A," and adds the next letter in the alphabet sequence, which is "B." For example, they would say, "A, B."
3. The game continues in this manner, with each player reciting the entire alphabet sequence in order and adding a new letter at the end. So, the third player would say, "A, B, C," the fourth would say, "A, B, C, D," and so on.
4. If a player forgets the next letter in the sequence, makes a mistake in the order, or takes too long to respond, they are out of the game.
5. The game continues with players reciting and adding to the sequence until only one player is left. This player, the last one standing who has successfully recited the entire sequence correctly, is declared the winner.

Tips:

- Start the game slowly and allow plenty of time for each player to recite their letter.
- To make the game more challenging, consider introducing variations. For instance, after reaching "Z," the sequence could start reversing from "Z" to "A," or players might have to recite the sequence backward.

45. Musical Memory

Number of players: 2 or more
Objective: To remember the lyrics from a portion of the song
being played

Instructions:

1. Begin by selecting a song to play. This could be a popular song that most people know or a new song to level the playing field.
2. Start playing the selected song and let everyone listen for about a minute or so. Make sure everyone pays close attention to the lyrics.
3. After a minute, turn off the song. It's important to stop the song at a random point to prevent players from memorizing only the beginning or the chorus of the song.
4. Each player must then try to remember and recite as many lyrics as they can from the portion of the song that was played. They can write it down on a piece of paper or simply say them out loud.
5. The player who remembers and correctly recites the most lyrics is the winner of the round.
6. You can play as many rounds as you like with different songs. The player with the most wins after a set number of rounds can be declared the overall winner.

Tips:

- To keep the game interesting, consider choosing songs from various genres and decades. This not only levels the playing field but also makes the game more inclusive and fun for people with different music tastes.
- For an additional challenge, you can ask players to recall specific parts of the song, such as the chorus or a particular verse.
- Introduce a speed round where players have less time to recall the lyrics.
- For a fun twist, players can be asked to sing the lyrics they remember instead of just saying them. This can lead to some hilarious moments, especially if someone is off-key!

AUDIO GAMES

Calling all music lovers — which is literally everyone! This lineup of audio games will have you grooving and guessing your way down the highway. You get extra points for weird looks from other road travelers passing by your retro dance moves!

First up, we're spicing up the classic "Name That Tune" by throwing some iconic TV show theme songs into the mix. Can you figure out the theme from "The Fresh Prince of Bel-Air" after just a couple of jiggy beats? There's no judgment for your rapping skills on this one.

Turn the passing landscape into your own personal zoo (besides the one in your car)! The "Animal Sound Game" will have you roaring…or clucking…or snorting. In this wild guessing game, players have to identify animals based on their unique sounds. But don't just stop with the easy ones. Cue your inner circle-of-life skills and try your hand with more obscure animals sounds (hyena, anyone?).

Get your ears ready and enjoy your ticket to ride!

46. Name That Tune (with TV show theme songs)

```
Number of players: 2 or more
Objective: To correctly guess the name of a TV show based on a
short clip of its theme song
```

Instructions:

1. One player will act as the game host and select a TV show theme song to play for the other players.
2. The game host will play a short clip of the theme song, usually around 10-15 seconds.
3. The other players will have to guess the name of the TV show based on the clip of the theme song.
4. The first player to correctly guess the name of the TV show earns a point.
5. The game host then selects a new theme song and the game continues.
6. The player with the most points at the end of the game is declared the winner.

Tips:

- Choose a specific genre for each round (e.g., '80s pop, country, movie soundtracks) to test your group's diverse music knowledge.
- Give bonus points if a player can continue singing the lyrics of the song after they've named it.
- If you're playing with a large group of people, it can be helpful to break up into teams to make the game more manageable.
- You can also add a time limit for each clip of the theme song to increase the difficulty of the game.

47. Animal Sound Game

```
Number of players: 2 or more players
Objective: To guess the correct animal that corresponds to the
sound played
```

Instructions:

1. The first player makes an animal sound, without revealing the name of the animal.
2. The other players have to guess the name of the animal that made the sound.
3. The player who correctly guesses the animal goes next and makes a different animal sound.
4. If no one can guess the animal after a certain amount of time, the first player reveals the name of the animal and play continues with the next player.
5. The game can be played in rounds, with each player having a chance to make a sound and guess.

Tips:

- To make the game more engaging, have players act out the animal as they make the sound.
- Introduce some less common animals into the game for an interesting twist.
- To make the game more challenging, players can limit the types of animals that can be used (e.g. only birds, only farm animals).
- For younger players, start with common animal sounds and progress to more challenging ones.

48. Guess the Song Game

Number of players: 2 or more
Objective: To correctly guess the name of the song that is being played

Instructions:

1. Select one person to be the "DJ." This person will be in charge of playing the songs.
2. The DJ plays a snippet (about 5-10 seconds) from a song. This could be from the beginning, middle, or end of the song, to keep things unpredictable.
3. As soon as the music snippet is played, the players must try to guess the name of the song. The first person to guess correctly gets a point.
4. After a song has been correctly identified, rotate the DJ role to another player. If there are only a few players, you can decide to keep one person as the DJ for a few rounds.
5. Continue to play until everyone has had a chance to be the DJ or until you reach a predetermined number of rounds. The player with the most points at the end wins the game.

Tips:

- To make the game more challenging, limit the number of clues the DJ can give or reduce the time limit for guessing the song.
- For an extra challenge, have players guess both the song title and the artist. You could give an extra point for correctly identifying the artist.
- If you don't have music available, a player could hum the tune while others guess the song.
- To make it more competitive, keep a scorecard and declare a winner after a set number of rounds.

49. 20 Questions (with songs)

Instructions:

1. One player chooses a song that they know well and keeps the name of the song a secret from the other players.
2. The other players then take turns asking yes-or-no questions about the song.
3. The player who knows the song can only respond with "yes," "no," or "I don't know" to the questions.
4. The players can ask up to 20 questions in total. Once the 20 questions have been asked, the players must make their final guess as to the name of the song.
5. If a player correctly guesses the name of the song before the 20 questions are up, they win the round. If not, the player who chose the song wins the round.
6. Players can take turns choosing songs and playing multiple rounds.

Tips:

- To make the game more challenging, limit the genres or eras that songs can be selected from.
- Use more obscure songs or lesser-known details about popular songs to make the game more challenging for music enthusiasts.
- If playing with a mixed-age group, consider sticking to popular songs that cross different generations to make the game more inclusive.
- Think carefully about your questions to narrow down the possibilities and make the most of your 20 questions.
- Players can agree on a time limit for answering questions to keep the game moving.

50. Music Trivia

Number of players: 2 or more
Objective: To correctly answer as many music-related trivia
questions as possible

Instructions:

1. Before starting the game, decide on the rules for asking and answering questions. You can use buzzers, hand-raising, or any other method that works for your group.
2. Choose a player to start. This player will ask a trivia question about music. The question can be about any genre, artist, or music-related topic.
3. The other players can then buzz in or raise their hands to answer the question. The first player to do so gets to answer the question.
4. If the player answers the question correctly, they get a point. If they answer incorrectly, the other players have a chance to answer the question and steal the point.
5. The game continues with each player taking turns asking trivia questions. You can set a time limit for each round or play until a certain number of points are earned.

Tips:

- To make the game more challenging, choose obscure or difficult music-related trivia questions.
- Consider dividing the questions into categories such as pop, rock, hip hop, etc. to make the game more organized.
- Use multiple choice questions for a larger group or to simplify the game.
- Allow teams to "steal" a question if the original team or player answers incorrectly.

51. Sing-a-Long

Instructions:

1. Choose a song that all players are familiar with and play it.
2. The first player starts singing along to the song. They stop singing mid-way through a line.
3. The other players have to complete the line by singing the correct lyrics.
4. The player who correctly sings the next line earns a point.
5. The game continues with the next player singing a line and the other players completing it.
6. If a player sings the incorrect lyrics, they lose a point.
7. The game continues until the end of the song.
8. The player with the most points at the end of the song wins.

Tips:

- Include songs from different genres and decades to keep things interest-ing.
- Try theme-based rounds, like songs about love, summer, or a specific

word.

- Encourage players to use props or enact the song to make the game more entertaining.
- Use a timer to limit the time each player has to sing their line.
- Consider giving bonus points to players who can harmonize or add a unique twist to the song.

52. Radio Roulette

Number of players: 4 or more
Objective: To find and identify as many songs or artists as possible by randomly selecting radio stations or streaming playlists

Instructions:

1. Divide the players into two or more teams.
2. Decide whether you'll be playing with an analog car radio or a streaming service. If using a streaming service, make sure you have a device with internet access and the necessary app installed.

For analog radio:

3. One player from each team takes turns scanning through the radio stations. Once a station is found, players have 10 seconds to identify either the song title or artist.

For streaming services:

4. Choose a pre-made playlist or create one with a mix of genres and artists. One player from each team takes turns hitting "shuffle" and playing the next song on the playlist. Players have 10 seconds to identify either the song title or artist.
5. If a player correctly identifies the song or artist within the 10 seconds,

their team scores a point. If not, the other team(s) have a chance to steal the point by providing the correct answer.

6. Play continues until a predetermined number of rounds or a set time limit is reached. The team with the most points at the end of the game wins.

Tips:

- Limit the time players have to identify the song or artist to 5 seconds instead of 10.
- Increase the difficulty by requiring players to identify both the song title and artist.
- Have players hum the tune or sing the lyrics to earn bonus points.
- Choose specific genres, decades, or themes to make the game more focused and challenging.
- Incorporate trivia questions about the songs, artists, or albums to add an extra layer of competition.
- Allow players to use "lifelines," such as asking a teammate for help or skipping a song, but limit these to a certain number per game.

53. Sound Charades

Number of players: 3 or more
Objective: To guess the word or phrase that the player is trying
to convey through sound without using any words or actions

Instructions:

1. The first player thinks of a word or phrase and then uses sounds to convey the word or phrase to the other players.
2. The other players must try to guess the word or phrase based solely on the sounds the first player makes. No words or actions are allowed.
3. The first player can use any sounds they want, including animal noises, musical instruments, and other noises.
4. If a player correctly guesses the word or phrase, they become the next player to convey a word or phrase through sound.
5. If no one can guess the word or phrase after a set amount of time, the first player reveals the word or phrase and starts a new round.
6. Play continues in this manner until all players have had a chance to convey a word or phrase through sound.

Tips:

- Encourage players to be creative with their sounds and use a variety of different noises to convey their word or phrase.
- Create categories of sounds, like "animal sounds" or "musical instruments" to keep things interesting.
- It can be helpful to set a time limit for each round to keep the game moving.
- To make the game more challenging, players can use more complex words or phrases or limit the types of sounds they can use.
- Give bonus points for extra creativity or particularly difficult sounds to guess.

54. Lyric Rewind

Number of players: 2 or more
Objective: To recall and sing the lyrics that come before the
section sung by the game master

Instructions:

1. Start by selecting a song that everyone in the car is familiar with. This could be a popular song from the radio, a classic from an old CD, or even a theme song from a famous movie or TV show.
2. The game master (GM), who could be the driver or a designated person in the car, will start singing the song from a random point in the song. They should sing enough of the song for the other players to recognize it.
3. As soon as the GM stops singing the other players' task is to "rewind" the song, meaning they have to sing the lyrics that come before the ones the GM sang.
4. If a player can sing the correct preceding lyrics they earn a point. If nobody can remember, the GM reveals the correct lyrics and no points are awarded for that round.
5. The game continues with the GM choosing different songs and starting points within those songs. The player with the most points at the end of the journey or after a predetermined number of rounds wins the

game.

Tips:

- To make it more challenging, the GM could pick less well-known parts of popular songs.
- The game could also be played in teams, with one person from each team taking turns as the GM for their team.
- If a player is unsure about the lyrics, they can ask the group for help or skip their turn.

55. Name That Band

Number of players: 2 or more players
Objective: To guess the name of the band or musical artist based
on clues provided by the other players

Instructions:

1. Choose a player to go first, and have them think of a band or musical artist.
2. The player gives a clue about the band or artist. This clue can be a song title, album title, lyrics, or any other relevant information.
3. The other players try to guess the name of the band or artist based on the clue.
4. If no one guesses correctly, the player gives another clue.
5. The player who guesses correctly gets a point and gets to go next.
6. If no one can guess correctly after a certain number of clues, the player who thought of the band or artist reveals the answer and no points are awarded.
7. Play continues until a predetermined point total or time limit is reached.

Tips:

- Encourage players to think of bands or artists that are well-known but not too obvious.
- Make the game more interesting by including solo artists as well as bands.
- For a challenge, use clues that reference less-known songs or facts about the band.
- Turn it into a speed round where the fastest correct answer gets the point.

56. Who Am I? (with celebrity voices)

Number of players: 2 or more
Objective: To guess the name of the celebrity based on their voice

Instructions:

1. Begin by selecting one player to be the "guesser." This person will be guessing the celebrity voices.
2. The remaining players (or one designated player if it's just a duo on the trip) will choose a celebrity to impersonate.
3. The chosen player will say a phrase or sentence in the voice of the selected celebrity. They can say anything, but it should not include direct clues like a catchphrase or a quote from a movie or show the celebrity is famous for. The purpose is to imitate the voice and speech style of the celebrity.
4. The guesser then attempts to guess which celebrity is being impersonated. They can ask questions that can be answered with a "yes" or "no," but they only get one chance to make their final guess for each voice.
5. If the guesser correctly identifies the celebrity, they score a point. If they don't guess correctly, the player who was impersonating scores a point.
6. Continue the game by rotating the guesser role among the players, or the impersonator if there are only two players. The game goes on until

everyone has had a turn to guess or impersonate, or until you reach your destination.

7. The player with the most points at the end of the game wins.

Tips:

- Choose celebrities that are well-known but not too obscure, so that everyone has a fair chance at guessing.
- To spice up the game, add a rule where the impersonator has to sing a song in the celebrity's voice if the guesser is having a hard time guessing. This adds a layer of difficulty for the impersonator and hilarity for the other players.
- If playing in a group, consider using a timer to limit the amount of time players have to ask questions.
- To make the game more challenging, limit the questions to a certain category, such as only asking about the celebrity's movies or TV shows.

OBSERVATION GAMES

If you've got a keen eye for detail and love to take in the sights around you, this chapter will be your road trip bestie!

Kick off your journey with the "Road Sign Game," a fan favorite that's perfect for staying in tune with the signs and signals of the open road. Your passengers will certainly appreciate that!

Feeling a little mischievous? Then you'll love the "License Plate Game," where you spot and decode different state license plates to create quirky phrases or words.

Got a car full of energetic little darlings? "Car Bingo" is a classic observation game that's perfect for group play. Keep your eyes peeled for items like road signs or vehicle types, and mark them off on your bingo card as you go. Whether you're cruising through bustling cities or lolling through the serene countryside, you'll find endless treasures waiting to be spotted and discovered.

So grab your fancy looking glass (or your regular glasses will be just fine), and let your inner Sherlock Holmes loose!

57. Road Sign Game

Number of players: 2 or more players
Objective: To identify the maximum number of road signs while traveling

Instructions:

1. Decide on a goal for the game: it could be to spot a specific sign or to be the first to spot as many different signs as possible within a specified time limit or distance.
2. If your goal is to spot specific signs, make a list of those signs before the trip starts. The list could include signs like "stop," "yield," "speed limit," a sign with an animal on it, a state welcome sign, etc. Everyone should have a copy of the list.
3. Assign points to the signs based on how common or rare they are. For example, "stop" signs could be 1 point, while a "falling rocks" sign could be worth 5 points because they're less common.
4. Every time a player spots a sign on the list, they shout it out and collect the corresponding points.
5. If you're playing the version where you spot as many different signs as possible, simply shout out when you see a new sign and keep a tally of the number of unique signs you spot.
6. The player with the most points or the most unique signs spotted at the

end of the game wins.

Tips:

- The "specific sign" version of this game can be customized for different trips. For example, on a trip to the beach, include beach-related signs on your list, like "beach access" or "no swimming."
- For longer trips, consider having "bonus rounds" where the value of all signs doubles for a certain period of time.
- To add a layer of challenge, you could include a rule where the spotters need to spot the signs in a specific order.
- If you have younger kids, provide them with pictures of the signs they're looking for to make the game more accessible to them.
- For an added layer of complexity, you could also assign negative points to certain common signs to make players more selective about what they call out.

58. License Plate Game (State Edition)

Number of players: 2 or more
Objective: To spot and call out license plates from different
U.S. states and territories

Instructions:

1. At the beginning of the trip, every player (or team) sets out to spot a license plate from each of the 50 states.
2. Each player should have a pen and a piece of paper to keep track of the states they spot.
3. When a player spots a plate from a new state, they call it out, and it gets added to their list.
4. The game ends when a player spots all 50 states or at the end of the trip.
5. The player who has spotted the most states wins.

Tips:

- Go even more old school and keep a printed map of the U.S. handy so players can cross off the states they spot, providing a visual representation of their progress.
- Introduce a point system based on distance. The further away the state is from your current location, the more points it's worth.

- Allow for bonus points if someone spots a license plate from a different country.
- To make the game more challenging, players can set a time limit or add rules such as not being able to count a state twice in a row.
- In case of a tie, players can play a tie-breaker round where they have to spot a specific state or find license plates with specific numbers or letters.

59. License Plate Game (Phrase Edition)

```
Number of players: 2 or more
Objective: To make a phrase or sentence using the letters found
on a license plate
```

Instructions:

1. At the beginning of the trip, every player (or team) sets out to make a phrase or sentence using the letters found on license plates.
2. Each player should have a pen and a piece of paper to keep track of the phrases and sentences they identify.
3. Choose a license plate that you see while driving or use one that you have seen earlier.
4. Using the letters on the license plate, create a phrase that relates to the letters or the plate itself.
5. For example, if the plate reads "FLY," a possible phrase could be "Flying Low Yesterday."
6. Another example: if the plate is "GTR 592," a player might say "Get The Rabbit."
7. Players take turns making phrases until everyone has had a chance to play.
8. Once all players have had a turn, award points to the most creative or funniest phrase.

9. The player with the most points at the end of the game wins.

Tips:

- If a license plate has fewer letters, players can use each letter multiple times to create longer phrases.
- Include bonus points for phrases that relate to your road trip or destination.
- Add a time limit for creating phrases after a license plate is spotted to increase the challenge.
- Introduce themes for rounds (like animals, movies, or food) to keep the game fresh.

60. License Plate Game (Observation Edition)

Instructions:

1. At the beginning of the trip, every player (or team) sets out to spot unique or interesting features on license plates.
2. Each player should have a pen and a piece of paper to keep track of the features they spot.
3. Players might look for vanity plates, plates from a particular year, plates with a certain number of identical digits, etc.
4. Players call out when they spot a qualifying plate, and the first one to call it out gets a point.

Tips:

- Players should keep their eyes peeled for different types of vehicles, including cars, trucks, and motorcycles, as each may have a different license plate.

- Customize the game for your trip by including specific items to spot (e.g., wildlife or landmarks for a national parks trip).
- Increase the challenge by requiring players to spot multiple unique features in a single round.
- For a more educational game, players could look for plates with numbers that are prime numbers, perfect squares, etc.

61. License Plate Game (Color Edition)

Number of players: 2 or more
Objective: To spot license plates of different colors and call
them out

Instructions:

1. At the beginning of the trip, every player (or team) sets out to spot different colors on license plates.
2. Each player should have a pen and a piece of paper to keep track of the colors they spot.
3. Decide on the length of the game and the color that will be counted. For example, you can choose to play for 20 minutes and count all the license plates that are yellow.
4. Start the game by announcing the chosen color. All players should start looking for license plates that match the color.
5. When a player spots a license plate that matches the color, they shout out the color and the state of the license plate. For example, "Yellow from California!"
6. The player who spots the most license plates of the chosen color by the end of the game wins.

Tips:

- To add a challenge only allow points for certain shades of a color or require players to spot a rainbow of colors in order.
- If colors are too easy consider adding other design elements to the challenge like a plate with a mountain or beach design.
- Remember the rarer the color or design the more points it should be worth to keep the game balanced.
- You can also play variations of the game such as spotting license plates from a specific state or with specific numbers/letters.

62. Movie Synopsis Game

Number of players: 2 or more
Objective: To guess the name of the movie based on a brief
synopsis given by a player

Instructions:

1. One player starts by thinking of a movie. They then give a brief and
   vague synopsis of the movie without revealing its title or any character
   names.
2. The other players have to guess the name of the movie based on the
   synopsis given.
3. If a player correctly guesses the name of the movie, they get a point.
4. If no one can guess the movie after a certain amount of time, the player
   who gave the synopsis reveals the name of the movie.
5. The player who guessed the correct movie or the next player in line
   then provides a synopsis for another movie and the game continues.
6. The game can continue for as long as the players wish to play.

Tips:

- To add a fun twist, make the synopses absurd or offbeat. For example, for "Jaws," you could say, "A seafood lover's vacation goes horribly wrong."
- To make the game more challenging, restrict the types of movies you can choose from (like only movies from the '80s or only animated movies).
- Set a time limit for guessing the movie to keep the game moving along.
- If the players are having difficulty guessing the movie, the player who gave the synopsis can give hints to help them along.

63. Spot the Car

Instructions:

1. One player starts by giving a description of a car they see on the road like a red sports car, a yellow truck or a police car.
2. The other players then try to spot a car that fits that description and shout out when they see it.
3. The first player to spot the car gets a point and then becomes the next person to give a description.
4. Play continues until a predetermined number of points or until the players decide to end the game.

Tips:

- Be specific with your descriptions to make it more challenging (e.g., "a red convertible sports car with a black top").
- For a longer game, players could choose rarer car types or colors.
- Consider setting boundaries for where players can look (e.g., only within a certain distance or on one side of the car).

- To add a strategic element, allow players to steal each other's car types if they spot them first.
- Consider incorporating license plates into the game for an added challenge (like spotting a blue SUV with a license plate that ends in a 5).

64. Car Bingo

Instructions:

1. Before the trip, create or print out bingo cards that include common items found while traveling by car such as road signs, vehicles, animals, and landmarks.
2. Each player receives a bingo card and something to mark off the items (like a pen or a marker).
3. The first player to mark off a row (horizontally, vertically, or diagonally) of items shouts "Bingo!" and is declared the winner.
4. To add some more fun to the game, you can create your own rules like a "blackout" game, where players have to mark off all the items on the card, or a timed game, where players have a set amount of time to mark off as many items as possible.

Tips:

- Use unique or funny car types or features (like a car with bumper stickers or a car with a roof rack) to make the game more engaging.
- To add difficulty, require players to take a photo of the car that fulfills the bingo criteria.
- For younger players, you can make the game easier by including pictures or simpler items on the bingo cards.
- It can be helpful to laminate the bingo cards or place them in a plastic sleeve to reuse them on future road trips.

65. Yellow Car Game

Number of players: 2 or more
Objective: To spot yellow cars while on a road trip and be the
first person to shout out "Yellow Car!"

Instructions:

1. The players decide on a time limit for the game, for example, 30 minutes
   or an hour.
2. Each player looks out for yellow cars while on the road and tries to be
   the first to spot one.
3. When a player spots a yellow car, they shout out "Yellow Car!" and earn
   a point.
4. The game continues until the time limit is up or until a predetermined
   score is reached.
5. Players can agree on any additional rules or variations to the game, such
   as specific types of yellow cars that are worth more points.

Tips:

- To make the game more challenging, only certain shades of yellow or
  specific types of cars (like only yellow taxis or yellow sports cars) earn
  points.

- Add a rule that you lose a point if you call out a car that is not yellow, to discourage guesswork.
- Include other elements like yellow buses or yellow road signs for additional points.

66. Counting Game

Number of players: 2 or more
Objective: To count from one to a predetermined number without getting interrupted or making a mistake

Instructions:

1. The first player starts by saying "1."
2. The next player says "2," and so on, until the predetermined number is reached.
3. Players take turns saying the next number in the sequence.
4. If a player makes a mistake, they are eliminated from the game.
5. The game continues until only one player is left, who is declared the winner.

Tips:

- Choose a number that is challenging but not impossible to count to. For example, 100 or 500.
- If a player suspects that another player has made a mistake, they can challenge them. If they are correct, the challenged player is eliminated. If they are incorrect, the challenger is eliminated.
- To make the game more engaging, implement rules such as counting in

multiples of a particular number, or counting backwards.

- For a more challenging version, try to count up using only prime numbers.
- You could also add a rule that players must also name something related to the road trip with each number (like 1 road, 2 trees, 3 cars, etc.)
- For younger players or beginners, start with a smaller number and work your way up as they improve.

67. Geography Game

Instructions:

1. The first player starts by naming a geographical location, like a country, city, or river; for example, "Los Angeles."
2. The next player must name a geographical location that starts with the last letter of the previous place named, in this case "Santiago."
3. The game continues with each player naming a place that starts with the last letter of the previous place named.
4. If a player cannot think of a place within a set time limit or repeats a place that has already been named, they are out of the game.
5. The last player remaining is the winner.

Tips:

- Set a time limit for each player to make a name to keep the game moving.
- Establish rules about what kinds of places are allowed (e.g. no repeating countries, cities only, states only, etc.).
- Make the game more engaging by allowing only certain types of

geographical locations like cities or countries.

- To make it more challenging require that the locations must be from a specific continent or country.
- For an educational twist have players share a fact about the location they named.

68. Alphabet Road Sign Game

Number of players: 2 or more
Objective: To spot road signs that begin with each letter of the
alphabet in order

Instructions:

1. Choose who will go first.
2. Starting with the letter "A," the first player looks for a road sign that begins with that letter.
3. Once a sign with the letter "A" is spotted, the player moves on to the letter "B," and so on.
4. The game continues until all 26 letters of the alphabet have been spotted in order.
5. The player who spots the most signs wins.

Tips:

- It may be helpful to have a list of the letters of the alphabet written down to keep track of which letters have been spotted.
- In case of a tie, the player who spotted all the signs the quickest wins.
- To make the game last longer, require players to find a set number of signs for each letter.

- For a more difficult version, have players find signs that contain, but don't necessarily start with, each letter.
- You can also add a competitive element by having players race to find each letter first.

69. Eye Spy Shapes

Number of players: 2 or more
Objective: To be the first player to correctly guess the shape

Instructions:

1. Choose a player to start the game. This player will choose a shape and say, "I spy with my little eye, something that is a (shape)."
2. Other players take turns guessing what the shape is.
3. The player who correctly guesses the shape gets a point.
4. The player with the most points at the end of the game wins.

Tips:

- Players can choose to play the game with specific colors or sizes of shapes.
- To make the game more challenging the shape could be combined with a color (like "something that is a red square").
- For more engagement restrict the game to certain categories of objects (like only road signs or only cars).
- To make it even more difficult consider complex shapes like parallelograms or rhombuses.

70. Alphabet of Objects

```
Number of players: 2 or more
Objective: To find an object that starts with every letter of the
alphabet in order
```

Instructions:

1. The first player starts by saying "'A' is for [name an object that starts with the letter 'A']."
2. The next player says "'A' is for [repeats the object named by the previous player] and 'B' is for [names an object that starts with the letter 'B']."
3. Each player takes turns repeating the objects named by previous players and adding a new object that starts with the next letter of the alphabet.
4. Players must name objects that are visible from their current location or from the car, depending on the agreed upon rules.
5. The game continues until players reach the letter "Z."

Tips:

- To make the game more engaging try to find objects outside the car for each letter.
- For more difficulty add a time limit for how long players have to find an object for their letter.

- To add an educational element have players say a fact about the object they chose.
- If playing with younger children, allow them to name objects that start with any letter instead of going in alphabetical order.

INTERACTIVE GAMES

These treasured games are designed to bring everyone together and immerse them in a world of fun. With a mix of hilarious games like "Mad Libs" and "Celebrity Heads-Up," and thought-provoking challenges like "Would You Rather" and "What If…?", there's a game for every car-bound comedian and philosopher (and everyone in between).

Expect lots of storytelling, imagination, and creative chaos as you try to guess movie titles, concoct absurd stories, or whip up witty rhymes.

These games will keep your travel crew entertained, engaged, and blissfully unaware of how many miles are left!

71. Mad Libs

Instructions:

1. One player, known as the "Mad Lib Master," creates a short story or finds a story or passage from a book. The story should have several words (preferably nouns, verbs, adjectives, and adverbs) that can be easily replaced with blanks.

2. The Mad Lib Master asks for the type of word needed for each blank (e.g., noun, verb, adjective, or adverb) without reading the story aloud. The other players take turns providing random words that fit the given type. The Mad Lib Master writes down the suggestions as they're given, filling in the blanks with the chosen words.

3. Once all the blanks are filled in, the Mad Lib Master reads the completed story aloud, revealing the hilarious and often absurd results.

4. Players can take turns being the Mad Lib Master and creating their own stories.

Tips:

- Encourage players to think of the most unexpected or outlandish words they can to create even more ridiculous stories.
- For an extra challenge, assign a theme to the story (e.g., road trip, beach vacation, or outer space) and require that all words provided must relate to the theme in some way.
- Incorporate words from billboards, license plates, or other sights seen during the road trip to make the game more interactive and relevant to your journey.
- If you're playing with younger children, consider simplifying the game by focusing on specific word types (e.g., only nouns or adjectives) or provide examples to help them understand what's required.
- For a competitive twist, have the players vote on their favorite completed Mad Lib story after several rounds, with the winner receiving a small prize or the title of "Mad Libs Champion."

72. Would You Rather?

Number of players: 2 or more
Objective: To ask and answer interesting questions and start
conversations

Instructions:

1. Have all players sit facing each other or where they can see each person.
2. The first player asks a "Would You Rather?" question to another player in the group.
3. For example, "Would you rather be able to talk with animals or speak all foreign languages?"
4. The player who was asked the question must choose one of the two options presented in the question.
5. After answering the question, the player who was asked the question asks another player a "Would You Rather?" question.
6. The game continues with players taking turns asking and answering questions.
7. If players cannot decide which option to choose, they can discuss and debate their options with each other.
8. The game can continue for as long as players want or until a predetermined number of rounds have been played.

Tips:

- Avoid common or clichéd situations and strive for unique, even bizarre scenarios.
- Encourage players to explain their choices. This can often lead to funny, heartfelt, or surprising revelations about each person, making the game more interactive and enlightening.
- When you're thinking of questions, consider the personalities, experiences, and tastes of the other players.
- To add a twist to the game, try including scenarios that could actually happen.

73. Truth or Lie

Number of players: 2 or more
Objective: To correctly identify whether a statement is true or false

Instructions:

1. Decide who will go first. The first player will make three statements about themselves. Two of the statements will be true, and one will be false.
2. The other players will then take turns guessing which statement is false. Each player gets one guess per round.
3. After all players have made their guesses, the first player will reveal which statement was false.
4. Players who correctly identified the false statement get a point. If no one correctly identifies the false statement, the first player gets a point.
5. Play continues with the next player taking a turn making three statements about themselves.
6. The game can be played for a set number of rounds or until a player reaches a certain number of points.

Tips:

- Mix in facts about yourself that they might not know, but aren't completely out of the realm of possibility.
- Be sure to include enough details to make it plausible. The more believable your lie sounds, the more challenging the game becomes.
- Whether you're telling the truth or a lie, try to keep your expression and body language consistent to avoid giving anything away.
- Use this game as an opportunity to learn more about your friends or family members.

74. Never Have I Ever

Number of players: 3 or more
Objective: To learn interesting and often hilarious facts about the other players

Instructions:

1. All players sit where they can see each other and decide who will go first.
2. The first player starts by saying "Never have I ever..." followed by something they have never done before.
3. For example, the first player might say "Never have I ever gone skydiving."
4. All other players who have gone skydiving would take a sip of his or her soda or put a finger in the air, something to signal they are in agreement.
5. Players who have not gone skydiving would not do anything.
6. The next player then takes their turn and says "Never have I ever..." followed by something they have never done.
7. Play continues in a circle until all players have had a chance to share.

Tips:

- Go for deep, thought-provoking, and funny experiences. The game is meant to help players learn new things about each other, so avoid being too general or vague with your statements.
- Don't forget to react to other people's revelations. This will not only make the game more interactive but also make everyone feel more engaged and connected.

75. Hot & Cold Word Game

Number of players: 2 or more
Objective: To guess the secret word based on given clues and
feedback

Instructions:

1. At the start of the journey, a player thinks of a secret word. They then give an initial clue related to it. This could be a single-word clue or a short phrase.
2. Players take turns guessing what the secret word could be based on the given clue. Each player can only make one guess per round.
3. After each guess, the player who thought of the secret word offers feedback in the form of "hot," "cold," or "warm."
   - "Hot" means a guess is close to the secret word.
   - "Cold" means the guess is far off.
   - "Warm" means the guess is somewhat close.
4. If no one guesses the secret word in a round, the player gives another clue, and guessing continues in the next round.
5. The game continues until a player correctly guesses the secret word. That player then gets to choose the next secret word, and the game starts again.

Tips:

- Use clues that can relate to multiple words. This adds an element of complexity to the game, making it more engaging and exciting.
- To make the game more engaging, the clues can be based on personal experiences or inside jokes that all the players would understand.

76. Storytelling Game (Interactive Edition)

Number of players: 2 or more
Objective: To collaboratively create a story by taking turns adding sentences or phrases to it

Instructions:

1. One player starts by saying a sentence to begin the story, for example: "Once upon a time, there was a young girl named Sarah who lived in a small village by the sea."
2. The next player adds another sentence or phrase to the story, for example: "She loved to collect seashells and would spend hours each day combing the beach for the prettiest ones."
3. Players continue to take turns adding to the story, each building on what has already been said to create a cohesive and interesting tale.
4. The story can go in any direction the players choose, so it's important to be creative and flexible in your contributions.
5. Players can choose to set parameters for the story, such as a genre, to make the game more challenging or interesting.
6. The game ends when the story has reached a satisfying conclusion, or when players decide to stop.

Tips:

- To make it easier to come up with stories, choose a theme for each round. It could be something broad like "adventure" or more specific like "magical creatures."
- Switch genres midway through the story for an unexpected twist, going from a mystery to a comedy, for example.
- Include a rule that each story must contain certain types of characters, like a villain or a wise old man, to stimulate creativity.
- As players take turns adding to the story, try to build off of what the previous player said. This will create a more cohesive and interesting story.
- Use props to add a layer of complexity to the story. The storyteller must incorporate whatever item they're holding into the narrative.

77. Headbands

```
Number of players: 3 or more players
Objective: To guess the word on the player's headband by asking
yes-or-no questions
```

Instructions:

1. Each player wears a headband with a word written on it, facing outward so that everyone else can see the word.
2. Without looking at their own word, each player takes turns asking yes-or-no questions to try to figure out what word is on their headband.
3. The other players can only respond with "yes," "no," or "maybe."
4. Players have one minute to guess the word on their headband.
5. If a player correctly guesses the word, they earn one point.
6. If time runs out and the player has not guessed the word, they can choose to keep guessing or pass their turn to the next player.
7. The player with the most points at the end of the game wins.

Tips:

- Try to ask questions that eliminate multiple options at once. For example, instead of asking "Am I a person?", ask "Am I an inanimate object?".
- Encourage players to ask open-ended questions to narrow down the

possibilities of what word could be on their headband.

- It can be helpful to establish a theme for the words on the headbands, such as animals, movies, or celebrities, to make the game more focused.
- When answering a question, consider acting out or miming answers to add a fun and challenging twist to the game.

78. Name That Movie

Number of players: 2 or more
Objective: To guess the name of a movie based on clues given by
the other players

Instructions:

1. Choose one player to be the "clue-giver" for the round.
2. The clue-giver thinks of a movie and gives clues to the other players. The clues can be anything related to the movie, such as actors, plot, genre, or quotes.
3. The other players try to guess the name of the movie based on the clues.
4. The first player to correctly guess the movie becomes the next clue-giver for the next round.

Tips:

- Describe scenes, talk about the actors, or mention notable soundtracks to vary the game.
- You can also play with specific categories, such as horror movies or romantic comedies, to make the game more interesting.
- For an additional challenge, try combining two movies into one clue. This forces players to think outside the box to figure out the clues.

- If players are having trouble guessing a movie, the clue-giver can give additional clues to help them out.

79. What If...?

Number of players: At least two players
Objective: To ask creative and thought-provoking questions that
lead to interesting discussions and debates

Instructions:

1. The first player starts by asking a "What If...?" question. The question can be anything, as long as it starts with "What If" and is thought-provoking.
2. For example, "What if you could have any superpower, but you could only use it for doing mundane tasks like washing dishes or mowing the lawn? What would it be and why?"
3. The other players take turns answering the question, trying to give the most creative and interesting response they can come up with.
4. Once all players have given their answers, the first player can choose the best answer, or the answer that they liked the most.
5. The player who gave the chosen answer then becomes the next person to ask a "What If..." question, and the game continues in the same manner.
6. The game can be played for a set number of rounds or can continue indefinitely.

Tips:

- Encourage everyone to think creatively and come up with unusual scenarios. The wilder the scenario, the more entertaining the responses.
- Try to ask "what if" questions that are open-ended and allow for different interpretations.
- Rather than just accepting an answer, ask players to elaborate on their responses.
- If players are struggling to come up with answers, give them some time to think or offer some suggestions to get the discussion going.

80. Rhyme Time

Number of players: 2 or more
Objective: To come up with words that rhyme with a given word
within a specified time limit

Instructions:

1. Choose a player to go first. This player will start by saying a word.
2. The next player must say a word that rhymes with the first player's word. For example, if the first player says "cat," the second player could say "bat."
3. Play continues in this way with each player saying a word that rhymes with the previous word.
4. Set a time limit for each turn, such as 10 seconds, to keep the game moving quickly.
5. If a player can't think of a word that rhymes within the time limit, they are out for the round.
6. The last player standing wins the round.
7. To make the game more challenging, you can set categories for the words, such as "animals," "foods," or "things found in a car."
8. Alternatively, you can make the game more collaborative by having players work together to come up with words that rhyme with a given word or phrase.

Tips:

- Set a rule that each word must be related to the previous word in some way (e.g. rhyming words that start with the same letter, words that are synonyms or antonyms).
- Encourage participants to think of phrases or full sentences that rhyme to make the game more challenging.
- Introduce a time limit to respond with a rhyme. The pressure of the ticking clock can make the game more exciting and challenging.

81. The Minister's Cat

Number of players: 3 or more
Objective: To come up with an adjective that begins with the next
letter of the alphabet

Instructions:

1. The first player starts by saying "The Minister's cat is an (adjective that starts with the letter 'A') cat."
2. The second player must then repeat what the first player said but with a new adjective that starts with the letter "B." For example, "The Minister's cat is a beautiful cat."
3. The game continues in alphabetical order, with each player coming up with a new adjective that starts with the next letter of the alphabet.
4. If a player cannot think of an adjective or repeats an adjective that has already been used, they are out of the game.
5. The game continues until only one player remains.

Tips:

- Shake things up by choosing a different theme for each round, like foods, cities, or movie titles.
- To make the game easier for younger players, you can limit the adjectives

to certain categories such as colors, animals, or emotions.
- To make the game harder for older players, you can require that the adjective also includes a certain number of syllables or has a specific sound pattern.

82. Celebrity Heads-Up

```
Number of layers: 4 or more
Objective: To guess the name of the celebrity that is written on
a card placed on your forehead
```

Instructions:

1. Make a deck of celebrity cards using index cards. Write a celebrity name on each card, then shuffle the "deck."
2. Choose one player to be the first "guesser" and have them draw a celebrity card and place it on his or her forehead without looking at it. Use a piece of tape or a hair clip to attach it.
3. The other players will give the guesser clues to help them identify the celebrity. The clues should only be in the form of "yes" or "no" answers to the guesser's questions.
4. The guesser can ask as many questions as they need to in order to identify the celebrity.
5. If the guesser correctly identifies the celebrity, they get to draw another celebrity card and continue guessing until they get one wrong.
6. The player with the most correct guesses at the end of the game wins.

Tips:

- Make sure to include a variety of celebrity types in your game - from movie stars and musicians to athletes and historical figures.
- When giving clues, encourage participants to impersonate the celebrity.
- To make the game more challenging, set a time limit for each guess, such as 30 seconds.

83. Movie Mash-Up

Number of players: 2 or more
Objective: To create a new movie plot by combining elements from two existing movies

Instructions:

1. One player starts by naming two different movies.
2. The other players then have to combine the plot and characters from both movies to create a new movie.
3. Players can take turns adding a new element to the plot, such as a setting, a character, or a plot twist.
4. The game continues until everyone has had a chance to contribute or until a designated time limit is reached.
5. Once the new movie plot has been created, players can take turns pitching the idea to the group.

Tips:

- Pick movies from entirely different genres to mash together. It forces players to be more creative with their mashup.
- Allow players to bring characters from one movie into the plot of the other.

- Challenge players to create a short "trailer" for their mashed-up movie, complete with taglines and dramatic pauses.

84. Time Travel Game

Instructions:

1. The first player starts by imagining a key event from history that they would like to change.
2. They explain what they would do to change the event and how they think it would affect the present day.
3. The other players can ask questions or provide feedback on the proposed change.
4. Once the first player has finished, the next player takes their turn to propose a change to another event in history.
5. Play continues in this way until everyone has had a turn.

Tips:

- Make the game more engaging by role-playing. When someone chooses a time and place everyone can act as if they're really there.
- Instead of just naming a place and time players must describe a specific event or scenario they would like to witness or change.

- Once a player chooses a time and place have them list the pros and cons of being there.
- Have a discussion about the possible consequences of changing the specific event or scenario.

85. Guess the Beat

Number of players: At least 2 players
Objective: To recognize the song by the beat, rhythm, or melody
tapped out by one player

Instructions:

1. One player, the "Rhythm Master," thinks of a well-known song and taps out the beat or rhythm of the song on a surface in the car (the dashboard, a book, their own hand, etc.).
2. They can tap the melody or just the rhythm of the song, but they can't hum or sing any part of it.
3. The other players listen to the beat and try to guess the song.
4. They can ask yes-or-no questions to narrow down their guesses, but the Rhythm Master can only answer with "yes" or "no."
5. The game continues until someone guesses the song correctly or the Rhythm Master has tapped out as much of the song as they can.
6. If no one can guess the song, the Rhythm Master can reveal the title, and a new Rhythm Master is chosen for the next round.

Tips:

- Introduce themed rounds where all the songs must fit a specific category like '80s pop hits or movie soundtracks.
- Besides guessing the song you can also include guessing the artist for extra points.
- You can make the game more challenging by limiting the number of questions players can ask or shortening the time limit.

86. Riddle Me This

Number of players: 2 or more
Objective: To solve riddles posed by the other players

Instructions:

1. One player thinks of a riddle. A good strategy for coming up with a riddle on the spot can be to observe an object or concept tied to your road trip, then describe it in an indirect, unusual, or humorous way.
2. For example, if you pass by a barn, your riddle might be, "I'm home to cows and horses, but you won't find any people living in me. What am I?"
3. Remember, riddles often involve metaphor, simile, and other figures of speech.
4. The player then states the riddle for the other players to solve.
5. Players take turns guessing the answer to the riddle. Each player can only make one guess per round.
6. If no one guesses the answer in a round, the player gives a clue to the answer, and guessing continues in the next round.
7. The game continues until a player correctly guesses the answer. That player then gets to pose the next riddle, and the game starts again.

Tips:

- To make the game fun for all players, select riddles of different difficulty levels. You can start with easy ones and gradually move to more difficult riddles as the game progresses.
- If the riddle is particularly hard, consider giving more than one clue or providing a multiple-choice set of answers to keep the game moving.
- To add a competitive element, you can introduce a scoring system. The player who solves the riddle can get a point. The player with the most points at the end of the journey wins.

CREATIVITY GAMES

We all have that one super creative person in the group, the one who is always drawing, writing, acting, and crafting something for us to marvel at and applaud. These creative games are right up their alley, and they're also fun for the less masterful among us.

Got a flair for doodling? Embrace your inner artist with the "Drawing Challenge!" Feeling like a paper-folding ninja? Tackle the "Origami Challenge" and see how many awe-inspiring creations you can whip up.

If you're craving an interactive experience, get ready to LOL with the "Improv Comedy Game." Or, channel your inner Hollywood director with the "Make Your Own Movie Trailer Game," where you'll compete to create the most gripping preview for a fictional film.

Whatever your creative cup of highly-caffeinated energy drink, we have the perfect game to keep your imagination soaring and your boredom at bay.

87. Drawing Challenge

Number of players: 2 or more players
Objective: To draw the best representation of an object or idea

Instructions:

1. Give each player a piece of paper and a pen/pencil.
2. One player starts by announcing an object or idea for the others to draw. For example, "Draw a cat wearing a hat."
3. All players have a set amount of time (e.g. 30 seconds to 1 minute) to draw the object or idea.
4. After the time is up, each player shows his or her drawing to the group.
5. The other players then vote on which drawing they think best represents the object or idea, without voting for their own drawing.
6. The player whose drawing gets the most votes wins the round and earns a point.
7. The game continues with each player taking turns announcing an object or idea for the others to draw.
8. After all players have had a turn to announce an object or idea (or after a set number of rounds), the player with the most points wins the game.

Tips:

- Implement a strict time limit for each round. This adds an element of pressure that can make the game more exciting and challenging.
- Have players draw something without looking at the paper or while wearing a blindfold. This is both hilarious and challenging.
- After a set time, have players pass their drawings to the person next to them to continue. This adds a collaborative (and often pretty funny) element to the game.

88. Songwriting Challenge

```
Number of players: 2 or more
Objective: To create an original song based on a given theme or
topic
```

Instructions:

1. Begin by choosing a theme or topic for the song. This can be anything from a specific emotion to a location or event.
2. Next, set a time limit for the songwriting process. This could be anywhere from 15 minutes to an hour, depending on how much time you have available.
3. Each player should then work on writing their own lyrics and/or melody for the song.
4. Once the time limit is up, players should come together to share their lyrics and/or melodies with each other.
5. Players can then collaborate to combine the best parts of each person's work into one cohesive song.
6. Once the song is complete, players can perform it for each other or record it to listen to later.

Tips:

- Give players a specific word or phrase that they must include in their song. This prompts creativity and can lead to some interesting lyrics.
- Challenge the players to write a song that combines elements from two distinct musical genres.
- Break the group into teams and have each team work on a verse of the same song. Then, bring it all together for a final performance.
- If possible, bring some musical instruments on your road trip (e.g. a guitar) to help players come up with melodies for their lyrics.
- If players are struggling to come up with lyrics or melodies, consider providing prompts or challenges to inspire them. For example, you could challenge players to write a song using only three chords or to create a song that tells a story.

89. Origami Challenge

Number of players: 1 or more
Objective: To create various origami shapes using only paper and folding techniques

Instructions:

1. To help learn folding techniques, research origami tutorials online or in books before you start your road trip. Maybe task someone on the trip to provide a demonstration to help spur creativity in the other players.
2. Decide on a specific origami shape for the group to create, such as a paper crane, frog, or butterfly.
3. Set a timer for a specific amount of time, such as 5 or 10 minutes, and challenge yourself or others to create as many of the chosen origami shape as possible within that time limit.
4. Once the time is up, compare the number and quality of the origami shapes created. The person who created the most and/or highest quality origami shapes wins the round.
5. You can also make the game more challenging by choosing more complex origami shapes or by adding restrictions, such as using only a certain size or color of paper.

Tips:

- Set a time limit for each creation. The pressure of racing against the clock adds a fun and challenging element to the game.
- For those who are inexperienced, select simple creations and add one small twist. Have fun watching each other struggle with the folding techniques.
- For those who are experienced with origami, try having them create a specific object without the use of instructions.
- Challenge participants to create something using a limited amount of paper or smaller sizes, which adds a level of difficulty.

90. Questions Only

Number of players: 2 or more
Objective: To carry on a conversation using only questions

Instructions:

1. Two players start the game. They can be in the front or back seat, as long as they can hear each other clearly.
2. The first player starts by asking a question.
3. The second player must then respond with another question that keeps the conversation going.
4. The conversation must continue with only questions. No statements are allowed. For example:
   - Player 1: Why is there a chicken crossing the road?
   - Player 2: Isn't that the punchline of an old joke?
   - Player 1: Don't you know any other jokes about chickens?
   - Player 2: Have you heard the one about the chicken who went to the library?
   - Player 1: Does the library allow chickens inside?
   - Player 2: Isn't there a rule that says only service animals are allowed?
   - Player 1: What services can a chicken possibly provide?
   - Player 2: Have you ever heard of an emotional support chicken?
   - Player 1: Is there such a thing as emotional support chickens?

- Player 2: Would you believe me if I said yes?
- Player 1: Are there other strange types of emotional support animals?

5. If a player responds with a statement, takes too long to respond, or their question doesn't logically follow from the previous question, they're out of the round.
6. Another player then takes their place, and the game continues.
7. The goal is to stay in the game as long as possible. The player who manages to stay in the game the longest can be considered the winner.

Tips:

- Assign a scene and characters to each player before they start the game. This gives them a specific role to play and can create interesting dynamics.
- Introduce random props that the players must incorporate into the scene. This forces them to think on their feet and can lead to some pretty funny situations.
- Use physical actions and facial expressions to add humor to the game.

91. Make Your Own Movie Trailer Game

Number of players: 2 or more
Objective: To create a trailer for a movie that doesn't exist

Instructions:

1. Divide passengers into teams or individuals. A two-person version can also work, with one person playing and the other judging.
2. Each player or team begins by brainstorming a unique movie idea. It can be any genre—romance, action, sci-fi, fantasy, comedy, etc.
3. Once the movie idea has been established, players then have to create a verbal or acted-out "trailer" for their imagined movie. This involves explaining the plot, describing the characters, setting the scene, and presenting the main conflicts or themes. They should try to make it as intriguing and engaging as possible, to draw in their "audience."
4. Players can use any items in the car as props or use different voices to represent different characters.
5. Each player or team takes turns presenting their trailer to the rest of the group. They can either narrate it in the third person like a traditional movie trailer, or they can act it out in character.
6. After all trailers have been presented, everyone votes on the best one. This can be based on creativity, humor, engagement, storytelling, and overall quality.

Tips:

- To add an extra twist, you can also provide a random theme, word or concept that must be included in their movie concept.
- Allow for some time for each team or individual to plan their movie idea and trailer before presenting.
- Have each team draw two different film genres and create a trailer that merges both.

92. Superpowers Game

Instructions:

1. The first player begins by saying, "I woke up one day and found that I had a superpower. My superpower is…" and they describe their superpower.
2. The next player continues the narrative by saying, "With that superpower, I decided to…" and they narrate an action or event that uses the superpower.
3. The next player can add a new twist like introducing a problem, a new character, or a new setting.
4. The story continues with each player adding something new while building on what was previously said.

Tips:

- Encourage creativity with the superpowers. They don't need to be traditional comic book powers. They could even be silly or absurd!
- To make the story more engaging, encourage players to add suspense, humor, and unexpected plot twists.

- Players can introduce new obstacles and challenges that the person with superpowers must overcome in order to save the day.
- You can also decide to play this game in rounds, where each round involves a new superpower and a new adventure.

93. Haiku Game

Number of players: 2 or more
Objective: To write haikus based on various topics and themes

Instructions:

1. Decide on a theme or topic for the haiku game, such as nature, love, or animals.
2. Each player takes turns choosing a word or phrase related to the theme, and everyone writes a haiku using that word or phrase.
3. A haiku consists of three lines. The first and third lines have five syllables, and the second line has seven syllables.
4. Once everyone has written their haiku, they read them aloud.
5. The group can then vote on the best haiku based on creativity and adherence to the form.
6. Repeat steps 2-5 for a few rounds or until everyone has had a chance to choose a word or phrase.

Tips:

- Turn the game into a competition where two players must create haikus based on the same word or theme, then have the rest of the car vote on their favorite.

- To make things interesting, players could be asked to describe a passing scene or object outside the car in a haiku.
- Provide a dictionary or thesaurus to help players come up with interesting words to use.
- Set a time limit for writing the haikus to keep the game moving.

94. Create a Bucket List

Number of players: Any
Objective: To create a list of things you want to do or
accomplish in your life

Instructions:

1. Have each player grab a piece of paper and a pen or pencil.
2. Set a time limit (e.g. 10-15 minutes) and have everyone write down as many things as they can that they want to do or accomplish in their lifetime.
3. Once the time limit is up, have each player share their top 5-10 items on their bucket list with the group.
4. Encourage players to discuss their goals and dreams, and offer support and encouragement to help them achieve them.
5. Consider making a group bucket list, where players can add goals that they want to achieve together as a group or on future road trips.

Tips:

- Assign categories such as travel, personal growth, or adventure and ask players to create bucket list items within those categories.
- Give each player a shorter amount of time (e.g., 2 minutes) to write as

many bucket list items as they can.

- Each player writes a bucket list item, folds the paper, and puts it into a hat. Players then draw a random item and have to guess who wrote it.
- Consider making a visual representation of the bucket list using items found in the car to keep everyone motivated and inspired.
- Remind players that a bucket list is personal and can include anything that is meaningful to them, no matter how big or small.

95. Paper Chain Story

Number of players: 2 or more
Objective: To create a collaborative story, one sentence at a
time, using only paper and pens

Instructions:

1. Each player takes a piece of paper and a pen.
2. The first player starts by writing one sentence at the top of their paper to begin the story.
3. The player then folds the top of the paper over, hiding the sentence they just wrote, and passes the paper to the next player.
4. The next player reads the last sentence written and writes the next sentence to continue the story, folding over the previous sentence before passing it on.
5. This continues until everyone has had a turn, and the story is complete.
6. Unfold the paper chain and read the story out loud.

Tips:

- Assign a genre (sci-fi, fantasy, mystery, etc.) to the story. This can help guide the plot and make the game more exciting.
- Set a rule that each player must introduce a new character into the story

during their turn.

- Encourage each player to end their part of the story with a cliffhanger. This makes it more challenging for the next player and adds suspense to the game.

96. Road Trip Scavenger Hunt

Number of players: 2 or more
Objective: To find and collect the items on the scavenger hunt
list while on a road trip

Instructions:

1. Create a scavenger hunt list that includes various items you might come across while on a road trip. Examples might include a red car, a state license plate from a specific state, a rest area with a playground, etc.
2. Distribute copies of the scavenger hunt list to each player.
3. Set a time limit for the scavenger hunt. This could be the duration of the road trip or a specific amount of time, such as one hour.
4. Players should keep their eyes peeled for the items on the scavenger hunt list and mark them off as they find them.
5. The player who finds the most items on the scavenger hunt list within the time limit wins.

Tips:

- Create a theme for your hunt, such as "wildlife" or "historic landmarks." This will help focus the search and increase engagement.
- Have players take photos of their finds. This not only provides proof

but also creates a fun photo album to look back on after the trip.

- Assign different point values to items based on their rarity or difficulty to find.
- Consider offering a prize to the winner of the scavenger hunt.

97. Paper Airplane Race

Number of players: 2 or more
Objective: To design and create a paper airplane that can fly the farthest distance

Instructions:

1. Give each player a sheet of paper.
2. Instruct the players to fold their paper into a paper airplane.
3. Once everyone has made their airplane, designate a starting line and a finish line in the vehicle.
4. At the same time, players should throw their paper airplane towards the finish line.
5. The player whose airplane travels the farthest distance wins the game.
6. Players can make adjustments to their paper airplane between rounds to try and improve its distance.
7. Players can have multiple rounds of throwing their paper airplanes to determine the overall winner.

Tips:

- Implement different design constraints for each round (e.g., it must be a certain size, fold no more than five times, etc.) to make it more challenging and foster creativity.
- Create obstacles or challenges in the car for players to navigate (just don't distract the driver).
- Have some rounds focus on distance (the furthest plane wins) and others on accuracy (hitting a specific target).
- Have different types of paper on hand, such as printer paper or construction paper, to see how it affects the flight of the airplane.

98. Rap Battle

Number of players: At least 2 players, but definitely fun with more people
Objective: To come up with the most creative and impressive rap lyrics on a given topic

Instructions:

1. Before the game begins, choose a topic for the rap battle. It could be anything from "favorite foods" to "famous celebrities" to "road trip destinations."
2. Decide on the order of play, time limits for each player's turn, and any other rules you want to establish.
3. The first player begins the rap battle by freestyling a verse on the chosen topic. The other players can either cheer them on or throw some friendly jabs to add to the fun.
4. Once the first player has finished their verse, the next player takes their turn, building on what the previous player rapped about or taking a new direction altogether. This goes on until everyone has had a turn.
5. After all players have had a chance to rap, the group can vote on a winner or simply enjoy the creative and entertaining rhymes that were produced.

Tips:

- Use props from around the car to incorporate into your raps. This can create humor and unexpected rhymes.
- To encourage collaboration, split into teams and have a group rap battle.

99. Tableau

Number of players: 3 or more
Objective: To create still images or "tableaux" that represent a
word, phrase, or scene, and have other players guess what they are

Instructions:

1. The game begins with one player thinking of a word or phrase. This could be anything from "beach vacation" to "angry lion." The more creative and imaginative the phrase, the more challenging and fun the game.

2. The other players will then use their bodies, facial expressions, and any props available in the car to create a still image, a tableau, that represents the chosen word or phrase.

3. They must freeze in their positions and cannot move or make any sounds.

4. This can involve positioning themselves in unique ways, making expressive faces, or cleverly using objects around them to add to the scene.

5. The player who chose the word or phrase allows the others a few minutes to examine the tableau. In this time, the observers must decipher the visual clues presented in the tableau and guess what the word or phrase is.

6. Once the word or phrase has been correctly guessed, the person who guessed it becomes the one to choose the next word or phrase, and the game continues.
7. The game keeps going in this manner, rotating the person who chooses the word or phrase.

Tips:

- Encourage players to be inventive in how they use their bodies and props to communicate the idea. They could form shapes with their bodies or use props symbolically rather than literally.
- To change up the pace, at times choose easy words or phrases to keep the game moving quickly. Other times, opt for more complex or abstract ideas to make the game more challenging and thought-provoking.
- Create a mystery theme by having one player think of a scene or theme. The other players then have to create a tableau based on their interpretation of it.
- Consider setting a time limit for guessing the word or phrase to keep the game moving.

100. Puppet Show

Number of players: 2 or more
Objective: To create and perform a puppet show using items found
in the car

Instructions:

1. Begin by gathering a variety of items from the car that can be used to make puppets. These can include socks, gloves, hats, paper cups, napkins, or anything else that can be safely and creatively repurposed.
2. Each player should choose a few items and start creating their own unique puppet or puppets. This part of the game encourages creativity and originality.
3. Once everyone has finished making their puppets, it's time to brainstorm a theme or story for the puppet show. This could be an epic adventure, a humorous comedy, or even a mystery.
4. The players then take turns performing their puppet show based on the agreed theme or story. The other players act as the audience and provide feedback after each performance.
5. After everyone has performed their puppet show, award prizes for the most creative puppet, the best storyline, and the most entertaining performance.

Tips:

- Make sure to pack extra materials that might come in handy for this game.
- Allow players time to prepare a script or an outline of their puppet show. Prepare some prompts ahead of time for players to use to get the creative process started.
- Encourage players to create unique voices and personalities for their puppets.
- Rotate roles between performances. If someone was a performer this round, they might be part of the audience next round. This can keep the game fresh and engaging.
- For younger travelers, modify this game to make it engaging and manageable.

  - Keep the story or theme simple. It could be based on their favorite cartoon, fairy tale, or a simple storyline that they can easily follow and participate in. For example, a lost puppet finding its way home, or a puppet learning about different animals.

  - If creating a puppet is too challenging, consider bringing along some pre-made puppets or simple sock puppets. They can still personalize these with markers or stickers.

  - Incorporate their interests into the game. If they love dinosaurs, make it a dinosaur adventure. If they love princesses, it can be a royal escapade.

BONUS: Burger Bet

Play a version of Lowen B. Hold's nostalgic game that inspired this book!

While Lowen is caught up in the nostalgia of his youth, he is aware of today's cost of burgers for the whole family.

So he modified the game to make your imagination front and center. This way, you can truly have your burger your way!

```
Number of players: 2 or more
Objective: To invent the most outrageous, delicious, or just
plain weird burgers you can think of
```

Instructions:

1. At the start of each round, one player will name a city or town you're passing through or heading towards on your road trip.
2. Each player then imagines they are a world-renowned chef in that town, tasked with creating the most inventive burger possible, one that truly represents the spirit of that location.
3. The players then take turns describing their imaginary burger, giving it a catchy name, and listing its unique ingredients.
4. For example, if the town is famous for its peaches, someone might create a "Peachy-Keen Bacon Burger."
5. After everyone has presented their burgers, everyone votes on their favorite creation. The player who designed the most popular burger wins the round.
6. The game continues with the next town, and a new round of imaginary burger creation begins.

Tips:

- This game is all about letting your imagination run wild. Encourage players to get really creative with their burger ingredients and descriptions.
- If you want to mix things up, you could change the food item each round. Maybe one round is about imaginary pizzas, the next about fantastical ice cream sundaes.
- Younger players can have fun thinking of wild, silly burgers, while older players might enjoy coming up with more sophisticated culinary creations.

About Lowen B. Hold

Lowen B. Hold is your road-trip maestro and living time capsule of a simpler era.

Imagine the charisma of the Fonz, the adventurous spirit of Marty McFly from "Back to the Future," combined with the eccentricity of your favorite uncle.

That's Lowen B. Hold, an emblematic figure that epitomizes the joys of a simpler time.

Growing up amidst the cultural vibrance of the '70s and '80s, Lowen recalls a time when life was celebrated on roller skates, big hair was a mark of style, and the soundtrack to life was a medley of pop-rock, disco, and the budding beats of hip-hop.

Summers were for spontaneous road trips with friends in a beat-up van, armed with nothing but a map, a Polaroid camera, and a well-worn cassette tape of their favorite mixtape.

The strains of Tom Cochrane and the Eagles, they believed, were the perfect accompaniment to the thrill of the open road.

Among the many cherished memories of Lowen's youth is the legendary road trip of '82, a quest across the states for the best cheeseburger in America, conducted from the comfort of a trusty Volkswagen Vanagon.

The companionship, the fun games like the inventive "Burger Bet," the laughter, and yes, even the few questionable cheeseburgers, culminated into a summer that still kindles warmth in Lowen's heart.

In an age where screen-time often usurps real-time interactions, Lowen nostalgically yearns for the joyous, predigital times.

His mission?

To reignite the flame of authentic fun in families, similar to those totally awesome rockin' days. His ambition lies not just in helping families and friends escape their screens, but in enabling them to savor the joys of the simple things in life and craft memories that outlast any device's battery life.

With a playful nod to the past and an embracing understanding of the present, Lowen's books invite you to embrace the nostalgia, laughter, and unforgettable memories that come with every turn of the page in his books.

Join the Road Trip Journey with Lowen B. Hold!

I'd love to see you join in the fun!

Visit my website at **lowenbhold.com** to stay updated on my newest books and adventures.

But don't stop there!

Connect with a fun community at **Facebook.com/LowenBHoldBooks.** Share your road trip pictures, videos, and moments of playing games from the book. If you have a copy of the book, let us see it in the photo!

Your shared adventures might inspire others to hit the road, too. Let's make every journey a cherished memory, together!